Dear Mom & All

Letters Home From Korea

by William Nace

TURNER PUBLISHING COMPANY

TURNER PUBLISHING COMPANY
Publishers of America's History

Editor: Randy Baumgardner
Designer: Peter Zuniga

Library of Congress Catalog No.
20021116394
ISBN: 978-1-68162-370-2
LIMITED EDITION

Dear Mother & All,

I am at Fort Meade, MD safe and sound after a long and tiresome train trip. We arrived about 6:00 p.m. yesterday, ate supper, received our bed clothing and haven't had to do anything since then.

Had a very nice trip and a good bunch of boys. There were only nine from Paducah left after two were put in the Marines and two others were sent back home. The rest were from Madisonville, Princeton, Murray and Bardwell. There was a total of twenty nine boys. At this time of the year the scenery in the Mts. was really beautiful. From the train all we saw colorful blanket had b... really something to see.

Last night and today I have found quite a few Paducah boys who are still here from the last call that have not been shipped out.

We will not receive our clothing until tomorrow. I'm kind of like Joe Ned; I will be glad to get some clean clothes even if it does happen to be the Army's. I even had to buy a towel a few minutes ago as I didn't bring one with me.

I don't know anything else to write at the present, but as soon as I find out anything I will let you know. In another day or so I am going to try getting a hold of Gene over in Baltimore as I suppose he will be there by that time.

Hope you can read this as I'm writing it on my bunk. Will write again real soon. As Joe Ned told you, don't write to me here.

Love,

Introduction....

Bill Nace and I have been friends since we started in the 7th grade in our hometown of Paducah, Kentucky in 1943. I had known his father, "Pappy" Nace, since 1937 when I started living with my Dad. Mr. Nace was a milkman who called upon both my Dad and Uncles' restaurants. He was a hard worker, but was always cheerful and laughing and kidding. He made me laugh in those strange and uncertain times for a little boy. I always felt close to him and that, no doubt, later made Bill and me close. It was not until I reached middle age that I realized that his nickname and his laughter and kindness to me were from his experiences of raising (with his equally kind and gentle wife) five remarkable sons. Just a few years after we graduated, Bill and I were inducted into the Army during the Korean War. The last time we were together and discussed what we were going to do with our lives was during that period. I was a military policeman on the west coast. Bill was an infantryman on his way to Korea. By daily one-day passes we were able to do what soldiers do on passes in Seattle for about seven days in 1951. It was a time of mixed emotions ranging from living life at its fullest to somber reflections on the future. Our lives after our soldier days were lived in different places in the country. There was college, marriage, children and work. He was in the ministry and college administration and mine in law, law enforcement and politics. We would meet at high school reunions and funerals of family and friends. All five of the Nace brothers earned college degrees and successfully made their way in their fields of endeavor. Bill, the middle son, has lived during, and can remember, the Great Depression of the 1930s, World War II, better times after the War, the Korean War as a soldier, college days, the deaths of his parents and friends, his work, marriage and children. His letters reflect on life some of those times and what he thought of the future at that time. Our lives for these 70 or so years was ordinary for the most part, but what made it an interesting journey was that we lived in extraordinary times. Bill sensed that. I hope you enjoy Bill's journey.

Albert Jones - May 2002

(Albert Jones has been an FBI Special Agent, State Prosecutor, United States Attorney, State Representative, and Mayor of Paducah, Kentucky. He is now retired.)

Bill Nace and Albert Jones in Seattle, WA, May 1952.

Dr. William H. Nace....

Dr. William H. (Bill) Nace is a retired United Methodist Minister, native of Paducah, KY and presently living in Jackson, TN. He is the third son of five sons of the late William M. and Lucille Green Nace of Paducah, KY.

He was educated in the public schools of Paducah, and is a 1949 graduate of Tilghman High School. Prior to being drafted into the Army in 1951, during the Korean War, he was employed by the Peoples National Bank and Trust Company of Paducah. He was sent to Camp Breckinridge, KY where he received sixteen weeks of heavy weapons basic training and eight weeks of leadership school prior to being sent to Korea in June of 1952.

When discharged from military service he entered Lambuth University Jackson, TN. At Lambuth he received a B.A. Degree and then entered Vanderbilt University Seminary for a Master's Degree. He is also a graduate of McCormick Theological Seminary, Chicago, where he received a Doctor of Ministry Degree.

Dr. Nace served as pastor of churches in Tennessee, Campus Minister at the University of Tennessee Martin, U.S. Army Chaplain, Tennessee National Guard, Vice President of Lambuth University, Jackson, TN, Vice President of Columbia College, Columbia, SC., Staff Member of the General Board of Global Ministries, Finance and Field Service, New York, NY and at the time of his retirement from The Tennessee Conference of the United Methodist Church was President of the Tennessee Conference Foundation of the United Methodist Church, Nashville, TN.

Bill and his wife Roanne live in Jackson, TN. They have one daughter, Paula Rushing and two granddaughters, Bailey and Abbey, all of Jackson, TN.

Dr. William H. Nace

Bill and Albert with little Pete and Lee III, the sons of Virginia and Lee Travis, May 1952.

The boys with Mrs. Lee Travis in Seattle, May 1952.

William H. Nace

Oct 4, 1951 - Owensboro, KY

2:15 p.m.

Dear Mom & All

We have just been sworn into the U.S. Army. I have been put in charge of all the boys and will be responsible for getting them to Ft. Meade, MD. We will leave here at 3:50 in the morning and will arrive at Meade somewhere between 8-11 o'clock Sat. Morn.

I no longer have Bill Smalley with me as he and 5 others were put into the Marines. They left just a few minutes ago. Hated to see him go, but glad not to go with him. I will let you hear from me when I reach Meade.

Love,
Bill

October 7, 1951

1:15

Dear Mother & All,

I am at Fort Meade, MD safe and sound after a long and tiresome train trip. We arrived about 6:00 p.m. yesterday, ate supper, received our bed clothing and haven't had to do anything since then.

Had a very nice trip and a good bunch of boys. There were only nine from Paducah left after two were put in the Marines and two others were sent back home. The rest were from Madisonville, Princeton, Murray and Bardwell. There was a total of twenty nine boys. At this time of the year the scenery in the Mts. was really beautiful. The trees were all turning and from the train all we could see were the tops. Looked like a large colorful blanket had been thrown over the mountains. It was really something to see.

Last night and today I have found quite a few Paducah boys who are still here from the last call that have not been shipped out.

We will not receive our clothing until tomorrow. I'm kind of like Joe Ned; I will be glad to get some clean clothes even if it does happen to be the Army's. I even had to buy a towel a few minutes ago as I didn't bring one with me.

I don't know anything else to write at the present, but as soon as I find out anything I will let you know. In another day or so I am going to try getting a hold of Gene over in Baltimore as I suppose he will be there by that time.

Hope you can read this as I'm writing it on my bunk. Will write again real soon. As Joe Ned told you, don't write to me here.

Lots of Love,
Bill

Oct. 12, 1951

9:15 p.m.

Dear Mother & All,

Just a few lines to let you know I am still living. Sorry I haven't written sooner, but to tell the truth I really haven't had the time. We finished processing yesterday, but don't imagine I will be shipped out before the first of the week.

Monday we received our clothing and believe it or not, all mine fit - even the shoes and combat boots. Tuesday we took tests all day which was pretty rough.

We had a total of ten of them. Wednesday we had a shot in each arm, received our dog tags, the hair cut and twenty bucks. Also we were interviewed and from what the classifier said, he thought he could fix me up in the finance office. Of course this doesn't mean I will get it, but here's hoping. You should have seen us after we had the shot in the left arm. They really got sore and stayed that way until today.

I am now getting up at 4:30 in the morning and marching about six blocks to the mess hall. This I don't care too much for, the getting up or the walking to chow line three times a day. Of course we have to make our own bed, which has to be perfect, clean up the barracks, wash our own socks and underwear and last but not least, when through with a cigarette tear it up, scatter the tobacco and roll the paper in a small ball and throw it away. Besides having to do all this, we all have had fun joking and caring on about these things. I have made a lot of good friends, and will hate to see us all have to break up before long.

I know this hasn't been much of a letter, but about covers what we have done this week. I am planning on calling home as soon as I find out where I will be sent. If it is not Camp Gordon, GA, I sure hope it's not too far from home. It is about time for the lights to go out so guess I had better close for now. Sure will be glad when I can receive some mail.

Lots of Love,
Bill

P.S. I have K.P. tomorrow for the first time, but don't imagine it will be the last.

October 19, 1951

Friday 7.30 p.m.

Dear Mother & All,

As you now know I am only about seventy five miles from home. I was very glad to get this close to home, but didn't care too much about the 101st Airborne. Of course this doesn't mean that I will stay in the infantry.

I was sorry I didn't get to talk to you the other night, but the main thing that I wanted was to give you my address, so I can receive some mail, which will be very welcome. This is really a nicer camp than I thought it would be.

I was the only one out of the thirteen which left Paducah and the sixteen that we met at Owensboro to be sent here. I'm telling you it was almost like leaving home again as I made so many friends. By the time we reached Meade, I knew most of the ones by name. As I told you I was in charge. Every single one of them would have given anything to come down here with me as most of them were from Madisonville and surrounding parts.

We arrived here about one o'clock Wednesday afternoon. There was a total of about two hundred sent from Meade to here. Of course after we arrived here we were again split up into different companies. There were eighty put in this Company, which is supposed to consist of heavy weapons. It is said to be the best outfit in the infantry. You even had to be qualified with a certain score on our tests to be placed in it. Of course this means sixteen weeks of basic, which will be pretty rough. Our basic will officially start Monday as they were waiting on another shipment of men from some other place to complete the Co. After basic I will more than likely go to eight weeks of leadership school, which is supposed to be a pretty good deal. As far as I'm concerned I had just about as soon spend my two years in this camp.

Yesterday we took another shot and was vaccinated. Also we had our identification cards made. Today, we were officially welcomed by the General himself. After this we were put on buses and given a tour of the camp.

I suppose I have about covered everything of interest, but will try to write more later. We just finished giving the barracks a good scrubbing for tomorrow's inspection. I still have to polish my boots and do a few odds and ends.

I hope you can read this as the only place we have to write is on our foot lockers. Anyway I think you will be glad to hear from, me, including mistakes and all.

Tell everyone hello, and I hope to be seeing you before long as after three weeks, we are supposed to receive a weekend pass.

Lots of Love,
Bill

Do I look proud to be a soldier or what? October 1951

Sunday

October 28, 1952 - 1:00 p.m

Dear Mother & All,

By now I imagine you might think I have forgotten about you or something, but not by all means. Believe it or not they have kept us busy doing something night and day, so like Joe Ned, Sunday is the only time I can find to write letters.

I received your first letter and last Sunday's paper Monday and also another letter the middle of the week, so therefore feel rather badly by not answering sooner. I have received two letters from Donna, and strange as it might seem a letter from Benton from a girl I don't even know. It was dated Oct. 19, but I did not receive it until Friday as it had only the 101st Airborne Division on it and had to have the rest of the address completed here. The only thing I could figure out, was that she must have copied it out of the Paducah paper. She said she just liked to write letters and hoped I didn't mind her writing me. I didn't mind at all, but was rather surprised to receive a letter in this manner. I let quite a few of the boys read it and they wanted me to answer it and send their names to distribute out among her friends. Guess I will have to do this as we all like to receive mail.

This is all the mail I have had up to date, but will be expecting quite a few letters this week as I wrote a few last Sunday. Yes, Joe Ned was one of the letters I wrote and am looking for one from him. Also wrote the Potts, Clovis, Ernest and Garland. Haven't heard from any yet. I was very glad to get Bill Smalley's address and will try to drop him a line this afternoon. Was so glad to hear you had been talking to Mrs. Smalley, as I know it will help you both.

About seeing me over the weekends, we will be eligible in two weeks for a pass, but doesn't necessarily mean that we will get one. The way this works, is that only fifty percent of the Company can be on pass at one time. You cannot have one if you are scheduled for K.P. or some other detail or if your barracks don't pass inspection. So you see what my chances are. I feel certain though that it will not be as long as it has been. I will keep my fingers crossed. If and when I do receive a pass I will not get home till sometime Saturday afternoon as a pass starts at

eleven thirty on Saturday and you have to be back by eleven o'clock Sunday Night. It will also be impossible for me to be home for the wedding as we have a GI party as we call it every Friday Night, which means cleaning the barracks for Saturday Morning inspection.

I know you were glad to finally get your chairs and by this time I guess Mr. Clark will have the papering done. Of course you really don't need the chairs now, like you did at one time, so you might as well have let them go and saved the money. Ha Ha! Just kidding!

It seems that everyone is really getting fixed up for the wedding. I know dad looks nice in his blue suit, as I always did think blue looked good on him and I am looking forward to seeing Larry all spruced up in his outfit. He is becoming quite a grown up boy now wearing a tie and all. I know he also looks nice, but I do think he could see about writing me a few lines and letting me know about school and all. Tell him to keep on with his music because-some day he will be glad he did. I was always sorry he ever quit. I bet he is still hearing "shut that darn thing up," but keep on practicing anyway and make the best out of it.

I was sorry to hear about all the deaths that have occurred since I left. I knew Rev. Arberburn very well, as I knew him while working at the drugstore and he came in the bank quite often. I knew Rev. Lovan when I saw him. I was very much shocked at Horace Meyer's death and also that of A.E. Boyd as I knew them both. Of course Mr. Boyd was much older than Mr. Meyers, but seemed in good health. I hated to read about Mr. Bynum, but knew his condition was poor. I can't recall Mr. Thomas, but guess I knew him when I saw him.

It seems that Leo knows his way around Paducah quite well, or at least he knows where to find Larry if he can't make it all the way home.

No, I haven't seen any of the Paducah boys here. The only one I know of is Omar Willis and don't know where to find him. If you know any other Paducah boys that are here, I know, please let me hear about it and I will try to look them up. That is if I find time.

Last Monday I had my first K.P. We went into the mess hall at 5:00 in the morning and did not leave until 11:30 that night I really, had the dish pan hands as about all I did was wash trays. Thank goodness this only comes about every twenty two days or once a month. It isn't hard, but just the hours. You also have to keep busy all the time. This is the day that I received your first letter and paper. I didn't even have a chance to read them till I got off that night. Speaking of the mess hall, we do

have some good food here and plenty of it. I have even learned to like things I never did eat at home. You will hardly recognize me when I come home as I have gained seven pounds since being in the Army. It seems that the Army agrees with me, although I don't agree with the Army.

We have been issued our rifle, bayonet, helmet and liner and all the rest of the gear that goes along with it. Like Joe Ned, of these things I am not proud. They keep pressing the one thing for which these are used. But as you said if we will just keep faith in the Lord and obey and trust his Word all things will work out for those who do this. That is what's wrong with the world today and the reason these things have to be taught, although they are not His teachings.

Our basic starts tomorrow, but we have been doing a lot of drilling already. I only wish it was as close to being over as I am to starting into it.

I went to church this morning at the chapel closest to our Company. It was a very nice service and from some of the things the Chaplain said I know he is a Methodist. He made a very good and inspiring sermon. I am enclosing the bulletin and if you will I would like for you to keep it for me. The service followed very much the same procedure as the regular Methodist Church, although it is called the Protestant Service. The boy who sleeps in the bunk under me and one other boy in the barracks I have made friends with all went together. One is from Maryland and the other is from Middlesboro, KY whose father is a Baptist preacher. Most of the boys here are from Maryland, Penn., Ohio, Iowa and all Northern States.

Before I forget it, if anyone is still planning on going after Gene, have them to stop here if its on Saturday, Sunday or between five and nine o'clock on the week days. I will be easily found as I'm on the main entrance road. Just keep going down the road and ask anyone where "George" Co. 516th is. The building number is T-478 or the orderly room is T-480. Also any Sunday that you all would like to drive up you are welcome to do so.

You asked if there was anything I wanted you to send, I don't know of anything I need except some good hangers, but this can wait until I get home and can bring them back. I wish you would buy me some books of stamps and send them as the only ones we can get here are out of a machine. Whatever they cost, get a check cashed somewhere and

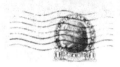

pay for them, my phone calls and also my church dues.

Believe it or not I am becoming quite a seamstress as I am having to sew on all my shoulder patches. They look good as some I have seen, so don't guess they look too bad. I am doing my own washing as we have a bendix machine in the barracks. It cost a quarter for nine pounds of clothes, so two of us usually go together and do a wash. We will get paid Wednesday and I am planning on buying an iron. We can buy a good iron at the PX for eight fifty and it will soon pay for itself as laundry costs two dollars a week and takes about a week to get it back. I know my shirts and things will never look as nice as if you had done them, but after a while maybe I can get the hang of it.

I suppose I had better close for this time as it seems I have done a lot of rambling and haven't said anything either. You will have to excuse the mistakes and all as I know there are plenty of them, and make it out anyway. This has been a rather long letter, but as I said I don't know whether I can write again before next Sunday or not.

Write every chance you get and encourage everyone you gave my address to, to do the same.

Lots of Love,
Your Son,
Bill

Postmarked - Nov. 5, 1951

Saturday Night - 9:15

Dear Mother & All,

This will have to be much shorter than my last letter, as I only have a few minutes before the lights go out. The reason I'm writing tonight instead of tomorrow, I will be on K.P. all day and will not have a chance. I really hate to pull K.P. on Sunday, but it just so happened it is my time and there isn't anything I can do about it.

I really enjoyed your two letters and the clippings. I was rather surprised to see B.J.P. announcement. Was also glad to see so much is being done towards better schools in Paducah. It was good to see Gene, Martha and Kenneth and I was glad to have met Lois - I believe was the correct name. I had even forgot about them planning on stopping. Short as the time was, I enjoyed the visit very much and hope they did the same. As soon as I knew they were on the way down I made a quick change of clothes and we went up to the milk bar - but suppose they have told you all about it. At any rate it was wonderful to get in an automobile once more, as like Joe Ned, it was the first I had been in since leaving home. The next time I see Martha and Gene it will be Mr. & Mrs. H.E. Nace, I believe will be correct.

I know the weather there is about the same as it has been here. You can tell Larry he wasn't the only one who got wet in that rain, as we were in it just about all day. Even carrying our rifles which we had to give a good cleaning afterwards. This was only the beginning as the last couple of days we thought we would freeze. It really gets cold drilling with that wind and snow hitting you in the face which we went through yesterday. I was really surprised at the snow this early in the year, but guess you had the same.

Yes, I would like very much for you to subscribe to the paper for me, if you will promise to let me pay for it. I don't have the least idea of things other than you write that are going on at home. This would help me very much if you would do so.

I had a letter from Bill Smalley and Garland this week. Bill said things were rather rough with him, but otherwise he is making it fine. Garland writes me that he is getting married January the 5th. This was

hard for me to believe, but guess you have also heard the news by now. In case you hadn't it is the girl who lives in Florida.

I have now finished one week of basic and only fifteen more to go. I have never seen a week fly by as fast as that one. This Army really has things mapped out, where they can run you through and at the same time put the point over. I am referring to the classes which we have had. I can say they have some good instructors who do their job well.

I guess I had better close for now before the lights go out. Tell everyone hello and I wish the best to the Bride and Groom. Hope all goes smooth for the wedding.

Lots of Love to all,
Bill

Eugene and Bill Nace, Bloomington , IN, January 1952

Dear Mom & All

Sunday - Dec. 9, 1951

11:00 a.m.

Dear Mother & All,

Just a few lines to let you know I am O.K. and hadn't forgotten you. I really enjoyed seeing Gene and Martha as short as the visit was.

In two hours we will be leaving on our long hike with pack and all, I only hope the weather will be nice this week as that will help out some.

Outside of having K.P. yesterday, I haven't done too much this week. Monday I was called to the orderly room to type all day. Tuesday morning I donated a pint of blood to the blood bank and therefore had the rest of that day off. It didn't bother me any at all. A few of the boys passed out afterwards. They were really nice to us, gave us orange juice, coffee and cookies afterwards. It was not compulsory to donate, but it really did me good, knowing that I might be helping to save someone's life. The blood is flown directly to Korea. Wednesday we had classes on the machine gun. Thursday I was barracks orderly which consist of keeping the barracks neat while the Co. is out. Friday morning again we had classes on the Carbine Rifle and had the afternoon off to see a football game between Breckinridge and Indian Town Gap, Penn. It was a wonderful game, Breck winning 13-7. So you see my week hasn't been rough and my cold is much better. I don't know what will happen to it this week.

As Gene probably told you I don't imagine I will be home Christmas or New Years, although there is a small chance. All but sixteen men will leave the 22nd of Dec. and return the 31st. This much time will be taken from their leave after basic, where as mine will be a gift from the Army from the 2nd of January until the 7th. I will also get out of that week of basic without having to make it up. Also during my ten days through 22-31, I can receive a pass any time I don't have duty. I will try to get home at least one day to see Joe Ned. I only hope I can make it Christmas. Despite the fact I may not be home for the Holidays I am getting a good deal from it giving me more time at home in the long run.

If you don't mind I wish you would send me an old telephone book so I can get addresses to address Christmas cards.

I guess this will have to be all for the present as it is time for chow and then its on my merry way for a week in the open. Excuse the pencil as my pen is in the bottom of my bag.

Lots of Love to All,
Bill

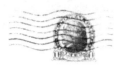

Robert Nelson, Earl Nagel, and Bill at Camp Breckinridge, KY, 101st Airborne, 1951

Tuesday Night

Feb. 12, 1952

8:00 p.m.

Dear Mom & All,

Just a few lines to let you know how much I appreciated you all bringing me back Sunday. I really enjoyed it all and hope everyone else did. I was sorry I didn't have more to offer and show you, but such is an Army Camp.

Yesterday and today we have had classes on the 4.2 inch mortar and will continue to have throughout the week. I mean a person really has to know what's going on to operate one of these, as there is so much mathematical problems to work out and solve. It is more or less along the line of surveying.

I am enclosing a picture one of the boys snapped at one of our so called G.I. parties. Bet you never saw me sling a broom like this before. I am not sweeping, but scrubbing the floor with soap and water.

It was really a beautiful day yesterday and most of today with the exception of a little rain this afternoon. I am keeping my fingers crossed about next week's weather. As fate will have it, guess it will be one of our worst weeks.

I wrote Joe Ned a few lines last night, but didn't think until a little while ago that he will have a birthday in a few days. Beings I don't have a card, I suppose I will write a few more lines and wish him many happy returns.

Mom, I haven't had a chance to get any valentines but will take this opportunity to send my love to the best Mother in the world and a mighty fine family of which I am proud of all. It is really wonderful to have a family where you think so much of each individual member.

I still have quite a bit to do before turning in so for this time I will sign off and will try to write again before bivouac as I won't have the chance out there. However, I will welcome all in coming mail.

Lots of Love to All,

Bill

P.S. I am now eating valentine cookies which one of the boys gave me. They are really tasty and decorated pretty.

Bill and friends at Camp Breckinridge, KY.

2:00 p.m.

Feb. 16, 1952

Saturday

Dear Mom & All,

Beings I won't have a chance to write next week, thought I would drop a few lines at this time.

Usually at this time on Saturday I would be about ready to head down that way. I would be today except for the fact that Donald Nelson, one of the boys you met the other night, and myself were the two unlucky guys picked to go out to the bivouac area at seven-thirty in the morning. The rest of the Co. doesn't go out until noon Monday. I guess I shouldn't complain too much as I feel rather guilty about having a pass every weekend when some of the rest were on details.

Yesterday I had three more shots and my arms are so sore I can hardly move them. We weren't scheduled to have these until next Saturday, but they sent a few of us up yesterday. Now I am glad I was one of them as they are now over with. As far as I know this will be all the shots I will have at Breckinridge.

Also, we finished up with the 4.2 inch mortar this morning. As I told you in my last letter, this is about all we have done this week.

There really isn't anything to write about, but just wanted to drop these few lines your way as there won't be anymore until next week.

I am enclosing these pictures, which are not any good of me. The other is of one of my good friends and his girlfriend taken when he was home Xmas.

Hope this finds all well and doing fine. Will be seeing you before too long a time, that's if I make it through bivouac and don't freeze to death. Just kidding, I will make it fine.

So long for this time,
Lots of Love to All,
Bill

P.S. I forgot to mention I received the valentines and appreciated them very much. I want to know if Larry addressed that envelope. I could hardly believe he has such a perfect handwriting. I tried to guess who it was from and when I saw brother on it, I still didn't know which brother could write like this. Was really shocked to find it was Larry. Keep up the good work kid!

Sunday Morning

March 9, 1952

9:15

Dear Mother & All,

Just a few lines to let you know that I am about to get settled in my new Co. and to let you have my address. I am writing this at the service club where me and two of my buddies have just finished coffee and donuts. We are planning to attend 10:00 o'clock church service.

I have really been busy trying to get everything in ship shape ready to start tomorrow morning. It is really going to be rough going and all I can do is my best. The way it looks I may not even have time to get home until my fifth week. Everything as I told you has to be perfect in every respect which will require lots of hard work and long hours.

We will work on a merit and demerit system being allowed fifteen demerits a week. This may sound like quite a few, but if you could see the things that you get them on it won't take long to add up to this total.

I hope you will be able to read this as I'm sitting on the arm of a chair and writing on a card table. I can hardly read it myself.

Well, this hasn't been much of a letter, but I will try to do better next time if I can find the time to write. Don't worry if you don't hear from me, because if anything is wrong I will let you know. The stripes which we will receive if making it through will be truly earned believe me.

Again, I want to thank you for a most wonderful time while at home and thanks a million for bringing me back. Hope you made it home all right and didn't make Dad too tired as he had worked all day. Hope this finds all well,

Lots of Love to All,
Bill

My address:
Pvt. William H. Nace US52154486
Co. "B " 42nd Tk. Bn. (Med)
101st Abn. Div.
Camp Breckinridge, KY.

Thursday

March 20, 1952

8:00 p.m.

Dear Mother & All,

It seems that I am finally getting around to writing a few lines. Not that I have any extra time, but think you deserve a portion of it.

I really, don't know where this week has gone. Tomorrow is Friday and I can hardly believe it. Suppose that it is because we have been so busy and haven't thought about the time.

I have given three periods of instruction this week and have made some fair grades. They try not to grade too high on your first periods of instruction so you will strive to do better on your next. After each period you receive a critique to find your faults. Taking all this into consideration I made good grades. Hope I can keep it up and do even better.

The duty roster was posted today and as I rather expected, K.P. Sunday. This knocks my weekend out of schedule.

Mother, I want to thank you again for all you did for us Sunday. I really enjoyed it and so did all the boys. They really appreciated it and had a wonderful day. Of course it was nothing to me to see the Kentucky Dam once more, but was a real treat for them. I hope we can all get together like that once more. These are our plans anyway.

Tonight we turned in our old horse blanket overcoats and received a new one which is very nice. It is on the order of Kenneth's trench coat and the liner can be removed making it into a nice raincoat. A fine time to issue them as tomorrow is the first day of Spring. Nevertheless, I am glad to get it and believe it or not, it fits perfect.

Last night on top of everything else, we had to GI the barracks as the General was supposed to come through today. Don't think he ever did. Tomorrow night it will be the same thing again for Sat. morning inspection.

Next week I have to give a fifteen minute talk on how to orient a map by using the compass. This will require a little study and preparation. I'm not too familiar with this myself.

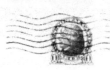

I suppose I had better close and get a little work done. As I told you, I will try to write as often as time permits. Hope this finds all well and doing fine.

Love to All,

Bill

Monday

March 31, 1952

5: 00 p.m.

Dear Mom & All,

First of all excuse the pencil and my not writing sooner, but under the circumstances you will understand. The fact is that I am in the hospital and have been for the past two days.

Don't be alarmed because it is nothing serious and I will get out tomorrow. I had my third diphtheria shot Friday afternoon which was a large dose and that night my arm began to swell and I became very ill with fever, chills and an upset stomach. I came to the hospital Saturday morning and when they found I had a temperature of 103.4 they put me right to bed in an isolated ward. (Why this ward I don't know, but they wouldn't let my buddies in to see me).

The Dr. called my case hyperpyrexia as a result of diphtheria toxic (whatever that means). If you recall I was sick the same way the week that we went to see Martha and Gene. This was right after I had my second shot of diphtheria, but didn't enter my mind being caused from this until it hit me again this time. Before I thought it was just the "flu" as it was going around at this time. I do however, recall my arm being very sore and red.

Saturday all they gave me was juices and water - plenty of it to get my fever down, also have been taking some kind of pills every three hours. Tonight was the first time they even let me go get my own meal. The rest of the time they have been bringing them to me. This I couldn't understand either, but such is the Army.

The Co. Commander brought my pay up here this afternoon and wanted to find out how I was and when I would get out. All the nurses and doctors have been very nice. Actually the only decent place I have found in the Army. At any rate I received a much needed rest, such as it was.

Leadership school is still progressing fine and so far all my grades have been passing. After this week and next we will have it pretty well made. As you know my PFC orders came through a week-ago today.

I had a very nice long letter from Joe Ned Friday. It contained just about all yours did or the last I read of his at home. Anyway, I was very glad to hear from him.

Mom, if you don't mind I wish you would call Wanda and tell her the reason I haven't written, but will do so when I get back to Co. and can find the time. Would write her also tonight, but I had to borrow this stationery, pencil and stamp from one of the boys here in the ward and I don't want to over do the thing. I also will try to write you a much better letter then.

Don't worry about me, as I'm feeling pretty well once more and will make it fine. Hope this finds all of you O.K.

Lots of Love to All,
Bill

Wednesday

April 7, 1952

10:00 p.m

Dear Mom & All,

Once again I will ramble a few lines to let you know that I am now back in the swing of things. I was discharged from the hospital about noon yesterday. I feel much better and everything is fine as can be.

I was very glad to have your letter waiting when I got here, but was sorry and shocked at the news it contained about the terrible accident. It was the first I had heard. I knew Mrs. Shelton and Mrs. Jones, beings as they both worked at Citizens Savings Bank. Of course I knew Mrs. Sanders and thought she was always so nice and friendly. It was a terrible thing to happen. I know all Paducah was shocked

I gave a troop information hour this morning on "Keeping Ahead In Research and Development." Beings as I had been in the hospital, I had to do most of my preparation last night and didn't think I was too well prepared. Much to my surprise I lectured the whole hour and came out with a big eighty-seven. Only a choice few were chosen to give these talks. They took the ones who had the highest grades on their other talks.

I was glad to hear Kenneth had gone to work with AEC. It sounds like a good deal and I know he will make the best of it. Hope it isn't too hard on him going to school and doing this too, but as you said, it will only be for a short while.

As yet I can't say whether I will be home for the weekend or not. Of course I will be there if at all possible. It is about my time to hit some detail around this place. At least don't wait up anymore. I was rather amused at your saying you were sure I was all right – If at the time you only knew I was in the hospital. Just kidding – don't ever worry about me and always trust I am all right, because if anything serious is with me, you will be the first to know.

I am sending a couple of pictures that were made the Sunday we went up to the Dam. We still have another roll to be developed.

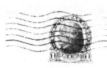

Mom, I guess I had better sign off and get a little shut eye. Here's hoping I see you at least part of the weekend

Trusting all is well and everyone is fine at home. I will close for this time.

Lots of Love to All,
Bill

P S. Don't answer this letter until you see if I make it home for the weekend

May 27, 1952

Dear Mom & All,

Just a short note and a few lines to let you know I spent part of last night in Chicago as you can see by the time.

We were supposed to have left here at ten last night, but the plane was grounded somewhere along the way on account of storms. At any rate the airlines put us up for the night in this swanky hotel fit for a king. If nothing happens we leave here at five this morning and are cleared as far as Denver. There isn't too much for us to worry about being late as I think we had a days grace and also a statement from the airlines as to why.

I called Gene while I was in Indianapolis and also Aunt Blanch after arriving here. Both seemed very glad I did. I would have gone over to Gary if I had known we were to be here this long.

Well, its time we were leaving for the airport. I will write more later. Goodbye for now.

Lots of Love,
Bill

May 29, 1952

Thursday 11:45

Dear Mom & All,

I have just returned from chow and thought I would throw a few lines your way. I may not finish it before formation time but will later.

As I told you in the card I wrote last night we arrived here Tuesday afternoon. I never thought an Army Camp could be in such a poor shape as we found this place. The so called barracks consisted of one floor. There is no latrine in the barracks, but one building which takes care of about four barracks. The camp as well as the city of Seattle is built on nothing but hills.

Mom, you can tell Mrs. Taylor I called the Travises Tuesday night and he seemed very glad I did. He wanted to know about everyone and the city of Paducah. I even talked to his wife and children which are three and four years old They wanted me to come out and have supper with them some night if I receive a pass. He said he would even bring me back to camp. As I told you in my card we had passes last night, but got a late start so I didn't go out. However, if I receive another one I am going to look them up.

Yesterday and today we have been processing and will continue to do so for two or three days more. We have an address which has to be put on the envelope, but don't write to me here as we don't know how long we will stay at this place. Not over a week

Well, I don't have to remind you of the fact that today I am a man. Like Joe Ned, one's birthday is just another day in the Army and I have to serve at the mess hall this afternoon.

I don't remember, but I think I told you about calling Gene while I was in Indianapolis. I just wanted to know if they got Joe Ned off all right and made it home without any trouble.

The days here are about the same as KY's, but the nights are real cool. Another thing it doesn't get dark until around 10:00 o'clock. They are on daylight savings time which makes us only an hour ahead of you.

William H. Nace

As I stated before, I will say goodbye for now.

Lots of Love to All
Bill

P.S. It is now 3:00 o'clock and I purposely left this unsealed until I went to the P.O. I received your letter and it was really welcomed. Was glad to hear all the news and I think you well covered it. Glad to hear Dad is cracking down on them up there and making them wake up to the fact that he is more important than they might think at times. – Ha.

Bob Wolff, Bill, Dewey Ross, and Earl Nagel, Camp Breckinridge, Spring 1952.

The four reunite in Charles City, IA, circa 1970's.

William H. Nace

Saturday

May 31, 1952

Dear Mom & All,

Once again I will write a few lines and strange as it may seem tell you what a wonderful time I am having in Seattle outside of Army life.

I told you about calling Lee Travis, so Thursday night when we got into town, I again gave him a ring and he wouldn't do anything but come down and take me out to his home. He is just like all the rest of the family, can't do enough for anyone. However, it seemed to do him as much good as it did me. We talked about everything and everyone he and I know in Paducah.

He has the sweetest wife and children anyone could possibly have. You will remember the picture Mrs. Taylor has of his two children. He also has a step daughter who is fifteen. All of them seemed to take right up with me and I felt like I had known them all my life.

They drove me around the city that afternoon (I say afternoon because it was still daylight) as I said before it doesn't get dark until 10:00 o'clock. After showing me such a wonderful evening they insisted I come out the next day which was Memorial Day, and we had off. I took them at their word and did just this, so last night we went to the stock car races which I enjoyed very much. His wife told me last night how much it really meant to Lee that I contacted them.

They both wanted me to come out again today, but I thought that was going too far. They did make me promise I would come out Sunday and eat with them, so I plan on this if everything works out.

Mom, I don't have the Taylor's address or I would drop them a line telling her how much I thank her for suggesting I call Lee. Be sure and call them which I know you will. Lee said that he didn't think there was a better person on this earth than Young Taylor, unless it was his wife Onabelle. Lee's wife said she had never met any of his folks outside his mother who came to visit with them, but she felt that Mrs. Taylor was just the person she would want to go and hug. I told her she would do just that.

On top of all this, when I got out of bed this morning one of the boys had a note for me from Albert Jones. He came to see me last

39

night, but of course I wasn't there. I called over at Ft. Lewis today, but they said he was in Seattle. Sure hope I get to see him.

I still don't know anything about when I will leave, but if its all right with you which I'm sure it is I will call home. I know you won't do it, but I will pay for the call. Speaking of expense, I forgot to pay my share of a florist bill while at home so write a check for whatever it might be - including yours.

I forgot to mention before, but the first day I was here I ran into Al Wilkerson. I kept hearing someone call "Nace" but couldn't figure who it might be. He came over where I was and we had a short chat. He also is going my way.

Mother, I really don't know anything to write except what a wonderful time the Travises have shown me. You may recall my saying about bringing some of the boys home with me from Camp Breckinridge that someday I wouldn't be so close to home and you and I would be repaid. This has already come true.

I want to give you their address and would appreciate it if you would write them a few lines expressing my appreciation for their taking me in. Also, if I am here longer than I expect to be I can hear a little from you this way.

Tell everyone hello and hope all are fine.

Lots of Love to All,
Bill

Lee's Address:
Mr. & Mrs. H.L. Travis Jr.
1433 30th Street
Seattle, Washington

Thursday

June 5, 1952

2:45 p.m.

Dear Mom & All,

While I'm not doing anything thought it a good time to give you the latest with me. First of all we were alerted and told when we ship.

We went aboard the ship Saturday morning and will be on our way. This really came sooner than we all expected. Everyone was glad of it as we all know we have to go anyway and want to get it over with. It will take us about two weeks before we hit Japan.

It sure was good to talk to you the other night. If I had of known we were going to ship so soon I would have waited a while about calling.

I think I told you about talking to Albert Jones on the phone and our planning to get together last night. Just as I expected I had detail and therefore we couldn't make it. I don't know if I will get a chance to see him now or not, but will do so if at all possible.

As I told you we are now living on a small Navy Base which they call Pier #91. It is really nice here and the food is the best I have had since being in the Army. I should have joined the Navy. Ha!

I have been a wondering what Larry is finding to do with himself now that school is out. Guess he is taking summer band and if he failed anything is going to summer school. Ha! I want him to write in his spare time when I get an address. I mailed a card this morning with my temporary APO on it. You can write me at that address and I will have mail waiting for me in Japan. There is no hurry as it will have two weeks to get there.

Guess yours and Dad's business will be picking up during the warm months. All I have to say is don't either of you work too hard.

Well, I don't know anymore news at the present time and don't imagine I will write anymore until we are over the way. I have been separated from Nelson, King and Nagel, but you remember Dewey

Ross who came down the night Bob Wolf's wife was with us. He and Bill Manley are still with me.

Tell everyone hello for me, that is all my friends who are interested. I will write again as soon as possible.

Lots of Love to All,
Bill

	NOTICE	INSERT DATE HERE
A SUPPLY OF THIS FORM WILL BE GIVEN TO EACH SOLDIER WHEN HIS ADDRESS IS CHANGED.	**CHANGE OF ADDRESS**	June 10, 52

MY NEW ADDRESS IS:

GRADE	FIRST NAME, INITIAL, LAST NAME	ARMY SERIAL NO.
PFC	William H. Nace	US52154496

COMPANY OR SIMILAR UNIT	REGIMENT, GROUP, OR SIMILAR ORGANIZATION
PROV Co SE-1363	

A.P.O. ADDRESS OR (Complete one only) → POST OFFICE ADDRESS OF INSTALLATION IN UNITED STATES

A.P.O. No. 613

% POSTMASTER

SAN FRANCISCO Cal

NOTE: WHEN THIS FORM IS SENT TO PUBLISHERS OF MAGAZINES AND NEWSPAPERS COMPLETE OLD ADDRESS BELOW.

SIGNATURE *William H. Nace*

MY OLD ADDRESS WAS: Co "B" 42ND FK BN CP BROCKINRIDGE, K.

WD AGO FORM 204
15 SEP 1944

This form supersedes WD AGO Form 204, 1 Nov. 1943 which will be used until existing stocks are exhausted.

49

WAR DEPARTMENT

OFFICIAL BUSINESS

PENALTY FOR PRIVATE USE TO AVOID PAYMENT OF POSTAGE, $300 (GPO)

MRS. W.M. Nace
1103 Greer Ave.
Paducah, Ky.

Monday

June 9, 1952

11:00 a.m.

Dear Mom & All,

To your surprise and mine also, I am still in Seattle at the pier. As I told you in my last letter I was supposed to ship Saturday morn.

Out of about three thousand which went aboard there were a hundred and seventy-five which they did not have room for. It just so happened I was in this small group. They lacked just six men getting down to me. Bill Manley was in the group ahead of me and of course got on. I imagine he will look the place over for me. I hated it due to the respect that I will have to go anyway and would have liked to stay with Bill. I don't know when I will leave now, but it will probably be this Thursday from what I have heard.

Although I did miss the ship I spent a wonderful weekend by doing so. By now I suppose you have received the picture of Albert Jones and myself. Yes, we finally got together last Thursday night and you don't know how glad we were to see each other - especially Albert. We went into Seattle and had supper. Albert was telling the waitress about our meeting and where we were from and she said her best friend lived in Paducah and told us the name of the place she was working here in Seattle. She told us the girl's name, but it didn't register to me who it might have been. We went down to see if we might accidentally know her and to my surprise it was Richard's former wife. I had only known her as she came in the bank when I was working there. Of course we recognized each other and she used to work in Albert's Dad's restaurant. It really was a coincidence to run into someone from home this way. She has been out here ever since she and Richard were separated. She really was glad to see us and of course it is nice to find someone from home this far away. It seems that I have been pretty lucky in this respect.

That isn't all I have met. Before I left home, Kenneth told me Bennie Arterburn was coming out here. He is in the Navy and has been here on the pier. I was going to chow the other day and ran into him. He came over to the barracks later and we had a nice little chat. He left the base

43

the same afternoon. I remember you saying you knew his father and brothers if I'm not mistaken.

Albert came over both Thursday and Friday nights and we really did enjoy ourselves. At the time I still thought I was leaving Saturday and told him so long on Friday night. Finding out Saturday I wasn't leaving, once more I gave him a ring which he was glad to get. He had the weekend off and stayed here in Seattle Saturday night with the Travises as they wouldn't have it any other way.

We went out there Saturday afternoon after calling first. Albert wanted to meet them and they Albert. They made us stay Saturday night which we had not planned on doing by any means. I don't think I told you but Lee had told me about Paul Hardy who has been here for a number of years and of course is from the land of Paducah. He is the age of Eugene and Charles and all their bunch. After Albert and I got there, Lee got in touch with Paul so he and his wife came out and we really did have a reunion. Paul really knew more of the people Albert and I know as he is a few years younger than Lee. Paul is an Uncle of Bob Hardy and his father is C.L. Hardy who is still in Paducah. I knew his dad also from the bank. It really is remarkable to find this many people so far away from home and ones you more or less know. Paul also married a Seattle girl after getting out of the service. Albert and I had better watch out - Ha? I don't think this could happen to us.

The mail is really fouled up around this place and I still haven't received any, through no fault of yours I know. I hope maybe I can get at least one before I ship out. Also, you have probably received that change in address card. I suppose that will still hold true, but you don't have to write to that one until I let you know something more. I imagine I have a letter somewhere to this address. By the time you receive this one more than likely I should be shipping.

I got to rambling and didn't finish telling about our weekend with the Travises. I had to come back Saturday night but they made Albert stay as he was going to get a hotel room. I left again Sunday morning and as we had planned I was to go back out there. Virginia, Lee's wife, had dinner for us and did it taste wonderful. She had fried chicken, cornbread, potatoes, green peas, gravy, salad and coffee. After we got through eating we watched TV for a while and Lee, Albert and I took the boys down to the beach which is on Lake Washington.

I think Albert and I enjoyed it more than his boys. From the beach

we could see Mt. Rainier which is sixty eight miles away. Mother, I have never seen a more beautiful scene than this. It looked just like a huge white cloud towering in the sky. This is really beautiful country. We went back, watched T.V. for a while and Albert and I left around nine thirty. As I have told you before it was still light at that time.

It really is wonderful the way they have treated me and Albert. I never was the one to impose on anyone, but they are the kind who always have their home opened to you and make and want you to feel at home which we both like to do. Albert said he had been out here sixteen long months and I was the first he had seen from home. Like we both told Lee and which they knew, it is wonderful just to get inside of a house for a change. I have only been gone two weeks, but it was still a treat for me also. His wife said she wanted us to consider her as our sister, which I think we did. So much for all this.

The barracks where we are living now is over the day room for the whole base, so we really have it nice. All we have to do is go down stairs to see T.V. make a phone call, read magazines or what have you.

Tell Dad the reason I mailed his Father's Day card early as I thought I was leaving and wouldn't have another chance. I will take this opportunity once more to say "Happy Father's Day" to the most wonderful Dad in the world.

Well folks, I think it is about time I signed off before I have to pay extra postage. I will try to write again when I find out what's what around here.

You might tell Mr. Willis that Albert and I ran into a guy that took basic with Omar and was a good friend of his. I don't remember his name, but think he was from Ohio.

Albert takes the *Sun Democrat* and he brought me over a bunch of papers. This morning I have been reading them and finding all the home town news. They had all the graduations in them which I enjoyed reading.

I was very much surprised last night when I went to send the telegram. They had a large sample copy of how to fill it out. We were only allowed to send certain messages and I thought the one I sent was the most appropriate. Back to the sample copy. What did it have but John Doe, 10 Jones Street, Paducah, KY. I don't know how

the old town got put on there, but it sure looked good to see it in this manner.

Well Mom, I think this about covers all the news for this time. I will try to write more real soon.

It is now 10:15 and I have just returned from personal affairs section. Here I made out an allotment of fifty dollars per month, which will be mailed to the bank and credited to my account. This will start the first of August. If at any time you need to check my account or write a check or any expense I want you to know you are free to do so.

This letter has covered a lot of time, but hope you find it interesting and a small amount of news. Tell everyone hello and trust this finds all well.

Lots of Love,
Bill

P.S. I almost forgot. It will come a little late, but Happy Birthday to a swell Mom. If I'm not mistaken it's also anniversary time - right. Let me know if I'm mistaken. Wish I could do something for you but will make it up later. They gave mail out on the train yesterday, but the only letter I received was from Albert Jones. Guess it all will catch me soon.

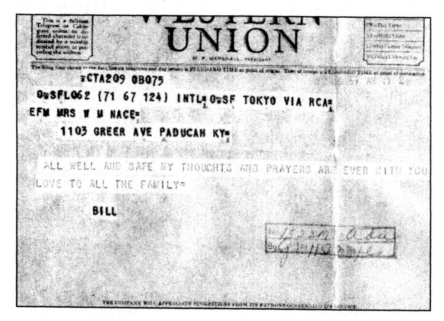

Wednesday

June 11, 1952

10:00 a.m.

Dear Mom & All,

This will have to be short, but just wanted to drop a few lines your way which will be my last from the U.S. for a while.

We will board the ship sometime this afternoon. It is really sooner than most of us expected.

I had a letter from Joe Ned this morning and was I glad to receive it. He told me about what had happened to his outfit as he did you also I suppose.

I called Albert again yesterday afternoon when I found out we were leaving today. He came over last night and we had a very good time. He knew where there was a nice Greek Restaurant and beings he's Greek also, Albert had the guy to fix us up with a big steak. He did this very thing and what a steak it was.

I called Lee last night to tell him I was leaving today. He told me about the letter he received from you, how much he appreciated it and also the wonderful way you expressed your appreciation for all they have done for me.

Well Mom, I don't know anymore news except it's pouring down rain. What a way to leave the U.S. I thought a letter before was going to be my last for awhile, so I will tell you again this one will be. Don't know how long the voyage will take, but will write you as soon as possible.

I don't think the change of address cards we made out before were ever mailed as we made out more yesterday with our APO. You can write me there and I will be looking for mail waiting for me in Japan.

This time you can tell everyone hello and goodbye for me. Take care of yourselves and everything else.

Lots of Love to All,
Bill

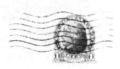

Sunday Aft.

June 15, 1952

1:45 p.m.

Dear Mom & All,

You may be surprised to receive this so soon, but we are going by way of Alaska and I found out they will pick up mail there.

We came aboard the ship Wednesday, but did not leave until Thursday afternoon at three o'clock. We were what they call the advanced party of the ship and our group pulls all the guard duty and K.P. K.P. isn't too bad as we get all we want to eat and then again it helps to pass the time away.

We are on K.P. one day and off the next. In between each meal we have about a two or three hour break and get off about six o'clock at night. I really don't mind it, but had rather not do it.

The ship is really crowded. Besides the American troops, which I don't know how many there are, we also have three hundred Canadian Troops aboard.

As I said, first of all we are headed toward Alaska and believe me you can really tell it when going on top deck. It is just like winter up there. Every morning we have to stay up there while they inspect our quarters.

We are sleeping on nothing more than a piece of canvas tied on to iron railings. These run four deep and I'm on the very top. Here's hoping I don't get seasick. The ship is really doing some rocking at the present time and making my writing difficult.

The weather was really beautiful when we left Seattle. They had a band playing and we had a real nice send off.

Mother, this has been short, but wanted to drop these few lines before arriving at Alaska. We will be there for about three hours the way I understand it, either to let troops off or take more on. Don't know which.

Tell all hello and I will write more in the future.

Bill

Wednesday

June 18, 1952

7.15 p.m.

Dear Mom & All,

I won't get to mail this until we hit Japan, but nevertheless, thought I would write a little as we go along and then not have so much to do when we get there. I will try to keep you posted as to what happens from day to day.

Guess you received my short letter which was dropped off at Alaska, or rather a small island which is part of Alaska and called Adak. We stopped there last night about six o'clock and then left again this morning at five.

You cannot imagine the beautiful snow covered mountains we saw, most of which were volcanoes. The whole place was nothing other than mountains of rock and believe me it was cold and as a matter of fact still is, as we haven't gotten too far away yet. There was even a thin coat of ice on the deck. This is hard to believe in June, but guess that's Alaska for you. It has beautiful country, but I wouldn't want to be there. Didn't see a single tree as I said before it was all rock. Tell Larry we saw a few seals.

I went to church this morning and really enjoyed it. A Chaplain is on board and conducts a small service each morning. We sing a few hymns and he gives a short talk - more or less of a devotional

Last night I went to the movies. We have a regular film but of course it doesn't have all the conveniences of the shows we are used to. They have to show it on a sheet and change reels, but we enjoy them anyway.

Guess this will be all for tonight, but will add more later.

On board the USS General Patrick, enroute to Japan, 1952.

Sunday, June 22, 11:45 a.m.

Have just returned from chow and thought it would be a good time to add a little more to my letter.

I went to church this morning and we had a very nice service. I will mail you the bulletin. Also have been attending all the daily services.

Of course there hasn't been anything out of the ordinary happening on ship as we follow the same routine each day. However, we did lose one day, which was June the nineteenth. We went to bed Wednesday night and when we woke up the next morning it was Friday, As you know this is due to our crossing the International Date Line. Each of us received a certificate and a card for our billfold making us a member of the "Domain of the Golden Dragon, Ruler of the 180 Meridian." I am mailing the certificate to you and please keep it for me. They also held a ceremony on ship featuring King Neptune. I have run my watch back a total of six hours since leaving Seattle. Probably will run it back even more.

Guess this will be all for now and will add more at a later date.

Dear Mom & All

Thursday, June 26, 1952, 7:30 p.m.

Well as you probably know by now from the telegram I sent, I am at Camp Drake, Japan. We left Yokohama Harbor yesterday (at 2:30 p.m. and came this far by train.

Maybe you read about the typhoon they had here in Japan the first of the week. We felt it out on the ocean and believe me there were plenty of seasick men. I don't know how I managed, but made it all the way without this happening to me. The front of the ship was even going down in the waves. It was really pretty to see the waves, but not like that.

We arrived here at Drake about 6:00 last evening. It is a three hour train ride from Yokohama and is only thirty-eight miles away. We didn't get to bed until 12:00 last night and then up again this morning at four thirty. We did most of our processing last night and will finish today. We are supposed to be on orders today. I am waiting now to be called out to finish processing. We are scheduled to leave by tomorrow. They really run you through here.

Of course you already know just about anything I could tell you about Japan. There isn't a place to be seen anywhere that there isn't a shack or something growing. It is really crowded. Of course I had always heard this, but didn't feature it the way it actually is.

June 26, 1952

11:00 a.m.

Dear Mom,

Have already sealed the letter I just finished, but wanted to tell you, we just had mail call and I received your letter of June 18. No, I have not received the one you failed to put the APO on.

I really was glad to hear from you and it sounds that all's fine at home. No, the address I have now is not permanent, but keep writing me at this one until further notice. Yes, I do want the *Sun Democrat,* but wait until I get settled and receive another address.

I didn't recall this being the time of year Eugene went over. Was glad Virginia wrote you and I wish you would send her a handkerchief. I wish I could do something for them. I am going to write anyway.

I haven't had any of your hot weather yet, but am expecting it before too long.

Mom, don't get discouraged with your work, but don't let it get the best of you.

So long for now.

Love,
Bill

Saturday

June 28, 1952

7:10 a.m.

Dear Mom & All,

This will be short, but just wanted to let you know that I have received my orders and leave this morning at 8:30.

I am going to the Third Infantry Division in Korea. We leave here just like we came in. Go back to Yokohama Harbor by train and then get a ship into Korea. It will take about five days.

Last night we turned in all our clothes but fatigues, underwear and socks and were issued the rest of our gear. You remember Dewey Ross who has been with me all along. He is going along also.

King, Nagel and Nelson have not yet received any orders. There were only twenty three from this Co. called for the 3rd.

Well this is about all I have for now. Just keep writing at my same address until further notice. Tell all hello.

Lots of Love,
Bill

Monday

June 30, 1952

8:00 p.m.

Dear Mom & All,

Today, I set foot on Korea. We arrived in Pusan Harbor around ten this morning, but didn't leave the ship until around four this afternoon.

We are now at the 8042nd Replacement Section. It really isn't too bad here. We have tents to sleep in with bunks. However, we may leave tomorrow as they said the ones who had orders for a Division would leave within twenty four to thirty six hours or whenever they could get transportation to move us out.

I thought parts of Japan were filthy and had heard all the stories about Korea. You can believe them all to be true and it was hard for me to realize some of the conditions existing that I saw on the way here. It really is pitiful. We left the ship and were put on trucks to come here which isn't too far from the Harbor.

As I stated in my last letter, we left Drake at eight thirty Saturday morning and took a train back to Yokohama Harbor where we boarded the USNS *General A. W. Brewster* which was similar to the *Patrick* we came over on.

I pulled guard duty on the way over, but wasn't too bad. My shifts were from noon till four in the afternoon and the same hours during the morning. We got to sleep the time we were off. My post was on top deck and it really was nice out there during the night as a cool breeze was blowing all the time. Quite a few of the men slept out there as it was so hot below.

I forgot to mention in my last letter about Bill Manley. He got a job in the postal service at Drake and will more than likely stay there for a while. This was on account of his profile. He has a bad knee.

King, Nagel and Nelson all received their orders the morning we left and all three are going into the 7th Division. I was looking in my address book to find out what Division the Hill boy was in. His father gave it to me one day while I was down at the bank. I had forgotten what Division it was and much to my surprise it is the Third. I will try to contact him if possible.

Speaking of addresses there are a couple I would like to have. I forgot what Ray Powell's wife said his was. I would like to have it just in case I might ever get around to his territory. Also I would like to have Bobby Nace's. I promised I would write him and never did.

You will have to excuse the green ink as I had to borrow some and this is all I could find.

This is about all I have for now so guess I had better sign off and hit the sack. Hope all are well and doing fine. I won't receive any mail until I reach my outfit, but will let you know as soon as I do.

Love to All,
Bill

P.S. I got one thing out of coming to Korea. I don't have to use stamps - Ha!

Wednesday

July 2, 1952

Dear Mom & All,

Yesterday morning around ten thirty we left Pusan by a so called troop train. Arrived here at the Third Inf. Repl. Co. this morning at three o'clock. What a time to get here.

I can't say much for the train ride as it wasn't much. We had wooden seats and they became pretty hard after awhile. Also, we ate our first C rations on the trip, a whole meal in two cans. They tasted pretty well, but nothing like a good old home cooked meal.

This place is located just outside of Seoul. It is rather a large place, but consists of nothing but tents and the old Army cot to sleep on. This isn't too bad for summer and Larry would probably like it. Suppose he also is doing some outside shut eye.

We will be here about three days and from here will be assigned to our unit. Believe me, I am ready to get settled wherever and whatever conditions it might be.

At the present time the Third Division is in reserve and hope it will stay there as far as I'm concerned. They have been back now for four months. It is one of the oldest divisions in the Army seeing action in WWI and WWII. It has quite a history behind it. The patch is a blue square with three white stripes.

This is about all I have to write for this time. It isn't much but wanted you to keep up with me. It doesn't cost me anything to mail them, which, by the way, I will enclose the stamps I have for your use. Don't use the address on the envelope, but the old Prov. Co. S.E. 1363. I will get it sooner.

Love to All,

Bill

July 4, 1952

Friday

Dear Mom & All,

Again this will be short as at the present I have no news or anything to write. Anyway, I'm not doing anything at the present and a few lines won't hurt anything, especially when you can send them free.

Today is really hot and hard to realize that it should be a holiday. They don't mean anything in the Army. However, the Chaplain held an outdoor service this morning in accordance with Independence Day. It was really nice and I enjoyed it very much.

I am now the lone wolf of the boys from Breckinridge. As I told you all my bunch besides Ross were sent to other Divs. Yesterday, Ross and one other who have been with me all along were called out to stay here. Sure wish I had been, but no such luck. Somewhere I must get a good deal as it seems all has been against me thus far.

I should know by the first of the week where I will be going.

As I said when starting out this wouldn't be much and it hasn't been. This is about all the news I know that's worth while for this time. Maybe when my mail comes through I will have some answering to do. Doubt if I will get any until I am assigned. Tell all hello and hope everything is fine and all's well. I am doing fine outside of burning up.

Lots of Love,
Bill

P.S. Again I will say use my old address (Prov. Co) and continue until I let you know different.

July 6, 1952

Sunday 6:00 p.m.

Dear Mom & All,

Just a few lines to say hello, send you today's bulletin and let you know I received orders today. Really did have a nice service today.

I received my orders this afternoon and am going to the 9th Field Artillery Bn. I can't understand this as I don't know the first thing along this line. At any rate it beats straight Infantry. Such as the Army does though. You never know. I will probably leave here in the morning.

I will let you know my address as soon as I get settled. This I will be glad to do anyway. Goodbye for now.

Love to All,
Bill

July 9, 1952

Wednesday - 12:15 p.m.

Dear Mom & All,

Once again I will do with my few lines. Not that I know anymore, but guess you will be glad to receive a letter, even if there isn't anything of interest.

Of course it is still plenty warm here, but we have to work in the heat just the same. We have two crews on our gun. Switch back and forth every two nights. That is the crew that is on sleeps in the bunker next to the gun and the other in the tent. Sleeping isn't too bad as we still have our cots and air mattresses.

I think I mentioned our guns are 155mm howitzers. If you don't know what they are, just ask Larry as he can probably tell you. They can make quite a bit of noise when fired.

The food isn't too bad here either. We have a mess tent and also a tent with crude constructed tables to eat on.

You were talking about my letters going into detail and all of the things I had done and saw. That's what made them so long and from now on imagine they will be short as its going to be the same thing here over and over.

I will make some pictures sometime soon, but may have to send them home to be developed.

We have a good bunch of boys here, but as usual, do not care for the Army and waiting for the time to get out.

Well, guess this is it for now. Will have to save something to put in my next letter. Guess my mail will begin to straighten out once more now before long. Trust all are well and doing fine. I am feeling fine and getting as brown as you can imagine. Good fresh sunshine.

Lots of Love,
Bill

July 11, 1952

Friday 10:00 p.m.

Dear Mom & All,

Again there is nothing new with me as usual, but just wanted to drop in and say hello.

I received your letter yesterday written the twenty-fourth of June. Was really surprised to get it as I didn't think my mail would start getting here so soon as it has to go through so many channels till you get my new address.

I have done a lot of things in my life, but today was the first time I ever went to the river to take a bath. We have a truck that runs down there about every other day. Not bad in this hot weather. I really needed it too.

I went to the movie last night. Just have to go about five miles by truck. Of course it is shown outside. The name of it was "Big Trees."

Was glad to hear Larry and Leo have adopted a cat. Not surprised at Larry, but was at Leo. Tell Larry to be sure and write and tell me about his team and also the Chiefs.

Mom, if you don't mind, there are a few things I would like for you to send me. I need some more T shirts and shorts. I don't know, but think I may have left some shorts at home. Have Kenneth to pick me up about three of each. You can write a check or I will pay you someday. Also, some stationery. Some Air Mail envelopes and paper. Don't need to buy a box. Just paper and envelopes. Of course if you have the time I will appreciate anything to eat. Any canned goods that we can eat without cooking or anything else you might think of. Don't go to any trouble.

One thing about this Artillery, we get to ride instead of walk. We have a tractor, similar to a caterpillar which pulls the gun and has a place for us all to ride. Really get the dust though.

Guess I had better sign off and hit the bunk. It isn't too bad living underground. We have a radio and at the present time are listening to Japanese music. The only thing, we have to use candles. Everything is pretty nice and better than I expected. This may be the break I have been waiting for as things could have been much worse in my case.

I am feeling fine and hope to stay this way. Don't work too hard and hope the heat has let up and you have had some rain for the crops. Goodbye for this time.

Lots of Love to All,
Bill

Tuesday

July 15, 1952

Dear Mom & All,

Today once again I received some more delayed mail. Two letters and a card from you, a letter from Gene and Marty, one from Joe and one other. Really was glad to get them all as it had been a week since I last received any. Had quite a time reading them all as they contained so much news. My mail should be straightened out before long now and will only take about six days. How long does it take you to get a letter?

Was glad to hear my cablegram came at such an appropriate time and also on your birthday. Yes, I guess it was just meant to happen the way it did. Thanks for picking it up as I would like to keep it.

I wrote to Jimmy & Virginia while I was in Japan thanking them and Aunt Blanch for a wonderful time in Gary, so guess they have my Prov. Co. address. I will try to write them again soon or may hear from them.

It seems you had quite a nice birthday. Was so glad you went out and had dinner and things worked the way they did. Sorry I couldn't have been with you.

Sure hope the heat has let up some. It is very unusual for that part of the country to have weather like that, but seems as if everyone is getting their share. Tell Dad to take it easy and not work himself down. Also, you do the same.

Larry really has a snap on carrying papers now. He doesn't remember when we had to go all the way to town. Tell him to take it easy on those windows!

It is nice to know that so many people miss me at the bank. It makes me feel that I put something into my work there and made many friends. Mrs. Craig was always so nice and to ask about everyone.

I may have told you, but I also wrote Lee and his wife thanking them for making my stay in Seattle so nice and pleasant. I shall never forget them and hope to see them again if I go back that way.

Will say goodbye for now and will try to write more soon. Tell everyone hello! We have been getting your hot weather you had so long here. Glad it is cooler at home.

Lots of Love to All,
Bill

My new address:
PFC William H. Nace US52154486
Headquarters Battery
9th Field Artillery Bn.
3rd Infantry Div. APO 468
c/o P.M. San Francisco, Calif.

P.S. Well it seems if I have to add a few more lines. A fellow from one of the other Btry's brought some mis-sorted mail over and much to my great surprise in the bunch was a letter from you and Joe Ned, both written the same date, July 15th. They both contained my former Btry "B" address so I see I'm now receiving mail from the states in about six days.

Appreciated the clipping about the streets. I won't be able to drive when I get back there.

Evidently the Potts did not let you know Clovis was leaving as you said nothing about it. Still I happened to think there is probably a letter written to my Prov. Co. which I haven't received, written before this one. I won't begin to tell you about Joe Ned's letter as I suppose he has written you the same about seeing Clovis, and Bill Buckingham. He said Bro. Potts had written him telling about Clovis. I was afraid they wouldn't see each other. I should be hearing from Clovis as Joe said he gave him my new address. Joe's letter was six pages long and I enjoyed it all. As I said guess he had told you the same.

I think I had better close before I write a book. Goodbye again.

Friday

July 18, 1952 - 9:00 p.m.

Dear Folks,

Nothing much new with me as usual, but imagine a few lines are always appreciated as with me.

I had a very pleasant surprise yesterday when Jimmy Hill, the janitor's son at the bank walked up. Was I ever glad to see him and likewise he me. Albert gave me his address when I was home and when I found we were in the same Div. I wrote him a letter. He is located about a mile from here. We talked for about an hour and are going to try and get together again soon.

Also, I may get out of the gun section. I'm keeping my fingers crossed and think I have a pretty fair chance. This is a clerk typist job with Sl back at Bn. Hqts. Myself and another guy were called to the Btry Commander's tent and he asked if we would be interested in the job. Of course both of us jumped at the chance and went for interviews this morning. The First Sgt. called and told me I was to report down there in the morning. All I have to do now is make the grade. Maybe this is the break I have been waiting for. Sure hope I can make it as Bn Hqts is located about three miles behind us and living conditions will be much better. Will sure be glad to get off the gun.

I had a letter from Dyersburg yesterday and stated Clovis was leaving the 9th and by now I suppose is gone. I suppose he went to Ft. Meade and sure hope he and Joe Ned get together. Hated to hear he was leaving, but know he was expecting it.

Guess I had better sign off for now and write more later. Hope all are well.

Lots of Love,
Bill

July 21, 1952

Monday

6:00 p.m.

Dear Mom & All,

Once again I take pen in hand and tell you how welcome your letter of July 10th was. I also have some rather pleasant news for a change.

I think I told you about my having wind of an office job at Bn. Headquarters. At the present time I'm writing from that very place. This is the kind of work I have been trying to get into ever since being in the Army. It isn't any easy job by all means as there are a lot of headaches connected with it. However it beats anything I have had so far. Really glad to get out of the gun section.

This is located about three miles behind where I was before. I speak of an office job, but it is nothing more than a tent. I have my own desk and do mostly typing. I should be a pretty fair typist when I get out of this as everything has to be perfect. It may take me sometime to get on to it, but hope I will make the grade.

Also have electric lights back here. I will move into this tent where the office is as soon as the other guy moves out, which will be about a couple more days.

Glad to hear you had such a wonderful time at Mayfield, but hated it because Aunt Lulye wasn't feeling too well.

Along with your letter yesterday I received letters from Virginia Travis, and Bro. Potts. Really a nice long letter from Virginia and she told me about sending you some of the pictures we made. She also sent me a couple.

Bro. Potts told me about Clovis having to leave, but I had already heard this through another source. Hope they contacted you when they took him to Paducah. It was really a nice letter and he said he would be praying for us both and I know that he will.

In today's mail I received a couple more letters which I am going to answer tonight One was from Earl Nagel and the other from Albert Jones. Earl and Nelson both are with the 17th Infantry Regiment. From all indications they have it a little more rough than I do. I am very thankful I have been so lucky up to now. Albert was telling me about

the weekend over the fourth he spent with the Travises. Virginia had told me the same things that they all did and what a wonderful time they all had. She said every five minutes someone would say "I wish Bill was here." Albert had bought both boys a jacket and T shirt each. Also he took along with him two chickens. Sure wish I could have been there. Virginia also told me about the J.E. Paynes from Paducah giving them a short visit. Said they remembered me very well and I knew them both through the bank and Taylors. Virginia may have told you, but she thinks they are going to have twins around the 1st of Sept. I know they will be thrilled to death if this happens.

I found enclosed with Albert's letter the very same clippings you had sent me. The Hester and Veal wedding and also about Bill Buckingham. I thought this quite a coincidence. Appreciated him thinking of me in this way.

By the way, if you have already started the paper I would appreciate you having the address changed if you don't mind. All the mail for the 9th Bn. comes through the tent where I am working and the mail clerk holds mine out instead of sending it to "B" Battery. So far I still haven't received any mail addressed to "B" Battery, but should be starting anytime now.

If you keep things going the way they are now, you are going to have all seniority at the office. Don't burn that typewriter up.

Guess the "Old Chev" runs better now, but hated so much had to be done to it. You should buy a new one since there is so much money flowing around in the family - Ha!

Suppose I had better sign off and answer a few more letters. I won't receive them unless I write a few. I find your letters so welcome as they always contain so much news.

Tell Kenneth to go right on with his schooling and stay out of the service as long as possible. No matter what he might go into it is all the same. He will be just about through college by the time I get started. Better late than never I now see.

I don't understand why Billy Buckingham wanted to join the Army. Looks to me as if he should have waited. Suppose Gore, the recruiting officer from Lone Oak had something to do with it. The clipping stated they were going to OCS, but still have to take basic first.

The clipping about me was just fine and I don't think it could have been any better worded. You don't know how much I appreciated the

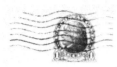

card and the message it contained. I know you meant it - Thanks!

The two pictures are very good and I will keep them. As I told you, would like to see the others, but might send them back home for keeping.

Things are still the same here. They are about to work us to death, but guess it will do me good. We keep going from the time we get up until dark and then some at night. There is always something to be done.

Of course I'm still taking my baths in the river and also washing my clothes. I realize how much your washing meant to me now that I do my own.

It is hot and dry here, but the nights are real pleasant -just right for sleeping.

I think this will have to be about all for now, but will write more soon.

By all means I am keeping faith in the Lord and all will work for the best as long as we do this. He is with me and all of us no matter where we are.

Lots of Love to All,
Bill

Friday - July 25, 1952 - 8:45 p.m.

Dear Folks,

Once again this will be one of those short letters, but like me, I know you always appreciate a few lines.

There hasn't been much happening around here since I wrote my long letter the other day. As usual there is a lot of work. I am getting the hang of my new job and think I will make it O.K. There is always some kind of a report to get out or some stencil copies to be run. Really keeps us going with all the rest we have to do. Each afternoon we work a little on a bunker we are building which eventually we will move into.

I had a nice letter from Bro. & Mrs. Potts yesterday. It really was nice as they both wrote a few pages and told me about Clovis leaving. I sure am anxious to know where he was sent. Hope maybe he was fortunate like myself and get somewhere he can make it home often. In the letter they wrote the church bulletin was enclosed.

I also had a letter from Albert Jones and he told me Bill Smally is on his way over. I wrote Bill a letter from Japan, but haven't had a reply as yet. Albert has really been nice to write.

It is still plenty hot here through the day, but is really pleasant for sleeping at night. I can always sleep no matter what conditions are.

There is a Korean kid here who has started doing my laundry for a small sum so this is one thing I don't have to worry about anymore. He does a much better job than I did too.

Well, this is about it for now so will say goodbye for this time. Mom, make some of the rest write and you not do it all.

Lots of Love,
Bill

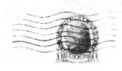

Sunday – July 27, 1952 – 8:30 p.m.

Dear Mom and all,

Just a few lines once again to let you know I received your most welcomed letter today containing the pictures. They were really better than I expected. I will send them back a few at a time so as not to make any one letter too heavy.

It rained all day yesterday, last night and most of today. This is what they call one of those Korean rains. I am beginning to see a little of that mud you hear so much about. I kept dry however as the tent did not leak.

I know you were glad to have Uncle James for a few days, but like you I don't see why some of the rest didn't come along with him. Of course it wasn't what you call a pleasure trip and they didn't know how long he would be there. Sure hope they get the thing settled so he will know what to do.

From the way you talk you must be doing all right with your pay-days. As I have said before and will say again, just keep it up as long as you can make out. Don't ever feel you don't deserve what is coming to you. Seems you are having quite a time keeping help, but such as the case with every one except the Army.

Gene and Martha also told me all about the convention on TV and said they were looking forward to seeing the Democratic Convention. I have just been wondering if there is any way I could vote in the Presidential election. Guess I would have to go to too much trouble to do so.

I am still doing fine and keeping well and also plenty busy. It seems the days are flying by but at the same time are going awfully slow. Today I received my first haircut GI style. I don't mean having it all cut off, but with hand clippers. A Korean kid did the operation and a pretty good job at that.

Well Mom, once again this has just been more or less of a note, but think you had just about as soon receive it a little at a time more often than longer letters further apart. At least it doesn't cost any more and is just as easy on my part.

Excuse any of many mistakes in the typing, but I am a little rusty and need the practice which is coming mighty fast.

Until next time tell all hello and be careful not to work too hard. I never have received that letter from Larry I told him to write. Tell him

he had better get on the ball and send me a few lines if he ever expects anything from me when I come home. Just a kidding him, but he can let me know about his many activities and Leo. Do you still have the cat?

Lots of Love to All,
Bill

P.S. I forgot to mention I had another letter from Bro. Potts yesterday and also the UPPER ROOM. He sure is a swell person to keep in touch with me and remember me the way he does. Of course they are still a little torn up about Clovis having to leave, but Bro. Potts mentioned how much he appreciated Joe Ned doing what he did. He sure thanked him for it. I was so worried all along that they wouldn't get to see each other. When you call also tell Bro. Turner I asked about him and say hello for me. I sure think a lot of him also.

Wednesday - July 30, 1952 - 9:30 p.m.

Dear Mom & All,

Well it seems that I was flooded with letters again this morning as I received six. Will never complain about this, although they all seem to come at once and I have quite a time getting caught up on my correspondence. Of course I look forward to yours most of all and try to answer them first. I received two from you, one from Jimmy and Virginia, one from Lois Simmons, Martha's cousin, and two or three others.

I was correct in thinking I had a letter from you addressed to the Prov. Co. that I hadn't received. It was written July 13th and contained the clippings of the Elliotts. I knew there was a letter somewhere telling me about Clovis leaving as I knew you wouldn't forget to send this news, although I had already heard it. I forgot about my hair in the pictures we took at the Travises. I never did mention it to you as I knew you didn't like it cut like this. However, here it is much better this way and I don't see anyone I care about seeing my hair. I will let it grow out when I get the great news I'm headed stateside, but this is too far away to begin to talk about now.

I appreciate your sending the address I asked for and also, Joe Duperries, although it is doubtful I will see him. You never can tell however, what chances you have meeting someone here and I will keep this address, just in case I'm lucky enough to get to Seoul someday. You inquired as to my whereabouts in the concern of a city. There aren't any cities around close or not much left of what do exist or have been. I am closer to Yonchon than any other place.

Sure thank you for getting a package on the way, but as you say it will be sometime before I receive it. Also thank Kenneth for fixing me up on the underwear. I'm sure the package will arrive in good condition as you always could fix them up nice. I am here where I see all the mail for the Bn. come in and I hate to see the condition some of the packages are in when they arrive. Of course they could have been fixed better in the first place. There is only one other guy and myself who sleep in this tent, so guess we can make out quite well on what you are sending. Glad you didn't put the envelopes and stationery in the box as I'm about out of envelopes. They are really scarce here as they stick together because of the heat and dampness. I have a small moisture proof bag I

keep mine in which helps out. In case you go a few days without hearing from me, I'm waiting on the envelopes.

I think I mentioned Bro. Potts told me Gene Williams was at home. Glad you got to see him and Bobby.

I appreciate you telling me about people asking about me, and as I said before it does me good to know I have such friends and people I wouldn't even think of remembering me such as Mr. Later.

Virginia, Jimmy's wife, certainly did write a nice long letter telling me all about their vacation. Six pages in fact. Told me about Jim's new job and his planning to go to school. She really knows how to write an interesting letter and I want to try and answer it tonight.

Speaking of the hot weather making Dad lazy - how is he, the grass and power mower making out? Haven't heard, but suppose it has helped him a lot. I don't blame him for being lazy and glad he is taking things easy through the hot months and want you to do the same.

It has been raining here for the past four days and nights and is still at it. What a mess things are in. Really seeing some of that Korean mud you hear about. Sure hope it lets up soon as things are getting bad for transportation purposes. I have kept pretty dry, except for the fact I had guard duty last night and slushed around through it.

Outside of all the rain everything is going as usual with me. Still busy as can be and keeping well.

I was quite amused at what you said in one of your letters about writing short ones and more often. I think I used about the same words in one of mine. I agree with this and will try to do the same.

Guess I had better bring this to a close for now and be hitting the sack as I didn't get much sleep last night. Hope all are well

Lots of Love,
Bill

P.S. Tell Mr. Hough I'm glad to hear I'm in his old Div. As I said before this Div. has quite a history behind it. If you see Jimmy tell him to drop me a line. What is he doing through the Summer?

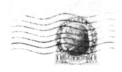

Saturday

2 August 1952

6:10 p.m.

Dear Mom & All,

Once again today, I was blessed with one of your most welcomed letters so won't waste any time about answering it.

As usual things are going on the same around here. I received a letter from Joe Ned today and much to my surprise one from Otley and Betty. Both were real nice letters and I especially appreciated the one from the Barbers. Betty said Martha had sent my address to them. Of course I will answer it right away.

Joe also told me about Bro. Potts calling him and said Clovis had left, but he didn't know where he was sent. It sure was nice of Mrs. Potts to write you a letter expressing her appreciation for what Joe had done.

Yes, I had heard from you know who that Melvin Carr had left the bank, but I do not know the reason why. Really was a shock to me as I thought he was all settled with his new home and all.

Sure hope you and the Taylors got to make the trip you had planned. Of course I expect to hear all about it if it came off as planned.

I had been wondering about Mama & Papa Nace and how they were getting along through the summer. Glad they are doing well and tell them all out there I said hello.

Was sorry to hear you had a few days of not feeling too well. Take it easy and as you said let some things go instead of making yourself sick.

Enclosed you will find a money order for $100. At last I am on the payroll again. Received $149.00 dollars yesterday. I thought it best to send some home as it isn't doing me any good here. If you find the time, or when you happen to be going to the bank, I would appreciate your putting it to my account. I had to send to the APO station to get the money order by the mail clerk.

William H. Nace

Well Mom, this hasn't been much of a letter, but a hello I imagine is always welcomed.

Be good, take care of yourself and tell all hello.

Lots of Love,
Bill

P.S. It quit raining yesterday after five days and nights, but has been at it again today.

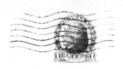

Tuesday

August 5, 1952

Dear Mom & All,

You cannot imagine how surprised I was to receive six letters in one from Bloomington, Ind. I really did appreciate the letters from everyone. It just seemed to start my day off right as I received it early this morning. Sure glad you got to make the trip and had such a wonderful time. Nice of all to contribute their bit to the letter. Tell Dad he will have to do this more often.

Another pleasant surprise today was a letter from Mrs. Richey. I have already answered it as it was so nice of her to think enough of me to write such a wonderful letter. You can also tell her how much I appreciated it. She told me all about the conditions at the bank and of her vacation. She also told me about your calling telling of me seeing Jimmy Hill and her passing it on to Albert.

Tell Mr. & Mrs. Taylor how much I appreciate their contributing to the letter to make it complete. Give me their house number and I will try to drop them a few lines. Guess you told them by now about Betty and Otley writing me.

There is still nothing to write about here as it's the same routine over and over. I hate to write a letter home anymore as I have no news of interest. I have been to the movie twice this week and of course this is always a good relaxation although the seats get pretty hard. Once again all the mud has turned to dust. It's always one or the other. I am still working hard and even at night. Like all jobs of this kind, there is more work to do at the last and first of each month than any other time.

This hasn't been much, but it is now 11:00 p.m. and guess I had better hit the sack. Just wanted to thank all for the letter I received today. Will have to wait until tomorrow to write Gene and Marty. Suppose they made it home this last weekend and all went as planned.

Tell Dad I will be glad to write Russel Mills if he will send me the address.

Until next time I will close for now.

Lots of Love,
Bill

P.S. The Lt. managed to get us a few envelopes today. He wouldn't even charge us for them. Believe me, the officers really have ways and means. He did this just for the ones here in S1. Nice of him anyway.

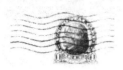

Friday

August 8, 1952

Dear Mom & All,

It is early in the morning to be writing a letter and don't imagine I will finish it before I have to go to work.

I was very glad to receive your letter of the 29th and hear about the remainder of the Bloomington trip. You must have been quite lonesome around home with Larry gone. I know he had a nice week and Gene and Martha enjoyed having him.

Yes, I feel that someone's prayers must have been answered for me to receive the position I am now in. As we all know those who believe and trust in the Lord all things will work out all right.

I have had letters from Mrs. Potts, Virginia Travis and Albert Jones since writing the other night. Of course they all were welcomed and very nice long letters. Mrs. Potts sent me Clovis' address and as you may have heard by now he is at Fort Lee, Virginia. This is Quartermaster's and they all seemed well pleased that he was there. He will have eight weeks of basic and then go to school for eight weeks. I have already written him as I know he too would like a little mail.

So glad you and Dad took time out for a movie. I have seen it advertised and Will Rogers Jr. picture. I will agree he looks quite a bit like his Dad. Maybe I will see the picture someday.

I suppose the "Bloomington Kids" as you call them had a nice weekend at home and hope all went well the way Martha had planned the shower. Bet Larry was glad to get back home.

There still isn't any news with me and about all I can do is to reply to your letters. This morning I have to go back to Special Services and pick up around 1500 donuts, enough for the whole Bn. You can bet I will get my share.

Albert sent me a picture he cut out of the *Sun Democrat* showing a speed boat on Lake Washington and Mt. Rainier in the back ground. The reason he sent it was that we were practically on that very spot the picture was taken when I was in Seattle. Suppose you remember seeing it, but in case you didn't pay any attention to it, I will throw it in this letter.

I received the stationery and envelopes day before yesterday and I sure thank you for them as I can sure put them to use. They arrived in good shape and I have already read the little book called the "Baptist Hour" you put in with them.

Well I have made it through with this letter such as it has been and get it in the morning mail. Hope all are well and I will write more later.

The mail clerk just handed me a letter from Ernest Walls which came back from "B" Btry this morning, so guess I had better close and read it.

Lots of Love,
Bill

Sunday - August 10, 1952 - 7:00 p.m.

Dear Mom & All,

Today I received a very nice hello from Leo. It was so nice of him to mail me a card like that. I think that was quite clever and I really appreciated it. I even showed it to some of the guys around here and they got a good laugh from it.

I was so glad to receive all the clippings, but I didn't realize the drought was so serious around there until I read them. I did enjoy the poem you enclosed which Leetha gave you and it had a very thoughtful message in it. I mentioned The Baptist Hour Pamphlet in one of my other letters, but didn't know where it came from at the time. As I said before it is so nice and thoughtful of people to think of me like this and it sure helps one to know you have so many friends who are interested in me. Hope to make it up to all of them someday. Tell Mr. Downen how much I appreciated his even thinking of me.

I think I told you already about Mrs. Potts sending me Clovis' address and I have written to him. I noticed you forgot to put his address in, but think nothing of it as I make the same mistakes.

I knew Martha's shower for Jackie couldn't have been anything but a success and glad everything went so well and she received so many gifts. Guess Larry really had a nice trip and a lot to tell.

Yes, I am still at the job, but like you say, not really enjoying it, but is much better than many other things. I think I can do as well here as most any place I could have been placed.

Sorry I didn't explain what a bunker was, but thought Larry would be up on these things. It has only become popular during this Korean War on account of the Country. Yes, it is much better than a fox hole and is usually dug in the side of a hill or mountain and reinforced with logs, sandbags or what have you. They are more or less a little hut upon completion and are better to live in during the winter months. We really haven't had the time to work on ours in sometime.

It is all right with me and I know it is with you also for any of the family to open my letters. I just address them to you, but they include all. Tell Larry I have some pictures I will send him if I ever get them developed. Speaking of pictures, sometime if you happen to be sending me a little package wish you would enclose some 127 film. Also some mug shaving soap as I can't get it here.

I was quite surprised to hear Val and Joe have adopted two children. I wouldn't have been so surprised at one as I have heard them speak about it before. Tell Kenneth to give them my regards the next time he sees them. They will make wonderful parents.

I really feel wonderful tonight as I had a chance this afternoon to go about seven miles and take a nice hot shower. Was it wonderful Crude, but it served the purpose.

Last night I went to the movie and enjoyed it very much. It was the kind you would have liked June Allyson in "The Girl In White," story of the first woman doctor.

Guess this about covers the latest with me so I will close for now and try to answer a few more letters.

Even if Dad doesn't write, it is nice of him to wash the dishes to give you the chance. I will consider this as making up for it - Ha!

Hope all are well.

Lots of Love,
Bill

Wednesday

August 13, 1952

Dear Mom & All,

Once again it is time for me to drop a few lines down your way, though I expect this to be another short letter with no news.

This was another day when all my mail hit me at once. It was quite amusing as you mentioned in your letter that I received six at a time and this is just what happened again today. Along with yours from Paducah I received one other, a nice letter from Clovis which I was glad to get, one from the "Bloomington Kids," Bill Smally and one from a girl in Iowa, Bob Wolff's wife gave my address to.

I want to tell you what Clovis said. He told me all about how nice Joe Ned was to him and went on to say, "I will always remember the Nace family as the nicest I have ever known." I really consider this something coming from him, and he said he was going to write you when he found the time.

I was glad to hear from Bill Smally, but his letter was written on the ship as he was on his way over here and I suppose is by now. I would appreciate it if you would call his mother and get his latest address for me. If I write to the one he gave me, it will have to go all the way back to the states, come back here and then go everywhere before catching up with him. I think he would get a letter much sooner by doing this.

Of course I always enjoy Gene and Martha's letters as they both write a little each time. They sure can write nice letters.

I enjoyed all the clippings you sent along. Seems as J.C. Dudley and his boys had quite a time. Sorry to hear about this. If I remember correctly the Lt. Col. had an accident while in before.

Looks as if you are getting your share of the mail also. I know it keeps you busy writing with all the rest you have to do. But the only way we will receive mail is to answer the letters we get. I will always try and answer the ones I receive as so far everyone has been so nice to write. Of course I put you first on my list and always answer them first.

As you say, we will try the paper for a month and see how it works out. With such a swell person as you to write so often I really don't need it as you tell me about all the news I would be interested in. Of course I

always welcome any mail coming from home, but don't want you to spend all your leisure time writing after a hard days work.

Think I mentioned in my last letter about going to pick up do-nuts for the Battalion the next day. The Sixty-fourth Tank Bn., that Bobby Gates is in and the boy Albert Hill's son told me about was on the road up that way. I stopped by on my way back and didn't have any trouble locating him. He knew me just us soon as I got out of the truck. We had a nice little chat and he said he would try to come over someday as it isn't too far. Also, when I returned I had a letter from Omar Willis awaiting me. Think I told you about my writing him to let him know where I was located and to find out about him. He really wrote a nice letter and it was sure appreciated. He wants me to send him Joe Ned's address and wants Joe Ned to write to him. I forgot to mention, the Gates boy left with both of them. I heard from Joe Ned yesterday and will try to answer his letter next, but I am on guard duty tonight and go on at nine.

This morning I attended church services and enjoyed it very much. Worshipping God in the outdoors and in a place like this can mean just as much and get the same thing from it as if you were in the largest and most lovely sanctuary to be found. It's the way you worship Him and not the place that counts. Our Chaplain is colored, but this to me makes no difference as creed, color and denomination has no boundaries here and we were all there for the same purpose. All this entered my mind as I sat there this morning and added so much to the service.

Well Mom, for a change I think I've written a pretty good letter although I may not have said much. I could add we went to the river again today and the water was really fine as it has been so hot. Couldn't compare with a beautiful Sunday afternoon on the shores of Kentucky Lake.

I didn't mention it, but had a nice long letter from Ernest day before yesterday. Between he and Mrs. Richey I have received all the latest from the bank. I am not hurting for mail and sometimes wonder if I can answer all I'm receiving, but as long as people are good enough to write I can always find the time to say, "hello."

Love to all,
Bill

Dear Mom & All

Thursday

August 14, 1952

Dear Larry,

I finally got some pictures developed so I'm sending them to you as you were disappointed about the others. I had to send them all the way back to Seoul to get them developed as a buddy of mine was going back there and he took them.

Gene and Martha told me all about your visit with them. Bet you really had a good time.

Well it won't be too long now before school starts again. I suppose you are ready.

I never did hear about what the Chiefs are doing this year. Do you ever go to any more ball games?

I forgot to tell Mother to do so, but you can buy Leo a can of dog food and give it to him for sending me his card. Tell him its from me!

Well old boy guess I had better be thinking about the sack. If you have the spare time drop me a few lines. I know you can do it. Be good and study hard when school starts. You will soon be looking towards High School, So long for now.

Your brother,
Bill

Sunday Afternoon

August 17, 1952 - 2:30 p.m.

Dear Mom & All,

Just received your nice letter which you wrote last Sunday, also the clippings and Church Bulletin. Anytime you can always throw the bulletin in as this way I can pretty well keep up with the Church and its activities, I am not too busy at the present time so thought this would be as good of time as any to answer. As I said before, we work just the same on Sunday, but somehow the work is never as heavy and everyone seems to be conscious of the fact it is the Lord's Day. Glad you received the money order all right and thanks for taking care of it for me. I can always depend on you for such things.

I'm glad you gave Jimmy Hough my address and he didn't waste anytime about writing as I had a nice long letter from him yesterday and have already answered it. He told me all about his summer. Sure was glad to hear from him. I also had a letter from Earl Nagel, as you remember from Baltimore and was home with me a few times. He doesn't have things quite as fortunate as myself, but is doing very well. He and Nelson are still together.

Speaking of the Turners asking about me, I intend to write them a few lines sometime real soon.

No, I didn't know Mrs. Wren personally, but do remember them. Sure was sorry to read of this.

The heavy rains we had are now long forgotten and the last three of four days the temperature had been around 116 degrees. This is really getting warm and I know I've never sweated so much in my life. Take plenty of salt tablets and make it fine. However, we do have a storm warning for sometime between 11:00 and 3:00 tonight. Sure hope it cools things off.

This doesn't sound right saying you enjoyed washing. I don't mean you ever complained about it, but I know it doesn't go too well after already doing a days work.

You may have told me about a new baby and I have just forgotten it, but who does it belong to, Laurine and Denton, or Hoffman and Maurine? You just said they had their children with them and I don't remember about the baby.

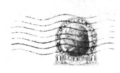

Yes, I am looking forward to the box any day now as it will soon be a month. Will make good use of anything in it. Will let you know soon as it arrives.

I had a very interesting experience yesterday, but one that is connected with a lot of work. There were two court-martials to come up in the Battalion and I was selected as the reporter. Of course I had never been through or did this kind of work before, but was given a good briefing on my duties and what to get down. I really felt funny with so many officers around, as you know they make up the court.

I hate to see and feel sorry for any soldier who is court-marshaled, but the Army has to have its laws and those who disobey must be punished. I spent the remainder of the day typing all the papers, forms, etc., and still have not finished with them. That's where the work comes in. It is really something to sit in at a Military Court and see how they operate. Of course we had classes on the Army Courts during basic and leadership, but never thought I would see one, much less be the reporter. I never want to be the accused. The Officers mess tent here at Headquarters served as the Court Room.

It is now 4:45. Our jeep was going down by the way of the showers and this was too good to pass up. It really felt wonderful and I feel much cooler and fresher. We take a bath whenever the opportunity arises to do so. I even drove the jeep. It felt good to get behind a wheel even if it happened to be a jeep.

Again this morning I attended Church Services and enjoyed it very much. It was really hot sitting out in the sun, but sometimes we have to make sacrifices such as this to do as the Lord would have us do.

Well, guess this will have to be all for now. Don't say your letters are not much, for no matter how long or short, they sure mean a lot to me.

Hope Larry and all enjoyed the pictures. Tell him to just keep them for me.

Love to all,
Bill

Headquarters, 9th Field Artillery Battalion, Korea

Thursday

August 21, 1952

8:30 p.m.

Dear Mom & All,

Was glad to receive your nice letter yesterday and also the envelope containing the news clippings. It was the first mail I have received since I got your letter last Sunday, the one you said you didn't mark air mail. I hadn't even noticed it and couldn't figure your sending Clovis' address and the piece of the church bulletin about the Smiths until I read the letter. Speaking of the mail situation, I didn't mean I was the only one not getting mail as there was none coming in on account of the weather.

Think I mentioned in my last letter about an approaching storm. There wasn't too much storming here, but we had some more of our hard rain.

There was no mail to come in the Bn. again today, but I should have quite a few letters on the way when the mail planes get back on schedule.

Last night I went to the movie. Had already seen it, but still enjoyed it as we find them such a relaxation. The name of it was "Rich, Young and Pretty" with Jane Powell and Wendel Cory. A couple of nights ago saw "My Son John," which was also right good. They run the same movie for two nights. This gives me a chance to see a movie one night and write letters the next.

I moved from the tent where I work into a hexagonal tent which sets on the side of a big hill. There are three of us in it, myself and two of the guys I work with. I made the change just to get out of this place at night. It really got tiresome working in the same place all day long and then sleeping there at night. I have to walk up and down a hill now, but don't think the exercise will hurt me.

Today I finally finished up the court martial papers I was telling you about. I made the remark if I ever get court-martialed, which I hope I don't, but would feel sorry for the guy who prepares the papers instead of myself.

Any day now I am looking for the package to arrive. If I recall it has been close to a month now and will probably have it all done away with by the time you receive this.

Well, guess this will have to be all for now as I don't know anything to write to waste another page. Hope all are well.

Lots of Love,
Bill

P.S. I just happened to think, this is Gene's Birthday. I wrote him and Martha about a week ago bidding them both a Happy Birthday. Believe Marty's was the 18th – Right?

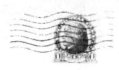

Saturday Night

August 23, 1952

9:45 p.m.

Dear Larry,

Boy, you really gave me a surprise when I received your very nice letter today. Guess you got mine about the same time I received yours. I will say you are a very good letter writer and can probably beat me. You will have to do this more often.

Seems that you are becoming quite a ball player. Just keep it up. Maybe before the season is over with North Side will be in first place. I will be pulling for you, but second place is really up there.

Last night I had guard duty once again, but didn't mind it too bad as I got to sleep all morning. About the time I hit the sack it started raining and has been at it ever since. This means some more of that Korean mud.

If it stops raining by morning, myself and one of the guys I work with are planning a trip of about sixty miles back to Seoul to spend the day. Beings it is Sunday and there won't be much doing, the Lt. gave his consent for us to go as there is a truck leaving early in the morning. If we get to make it will let you know all about the trip.

The Battery got a new radio to sell yesterday, so myself and the rest of the guys I work with all pitched in and bought it. We are now listening to music and really enjoying it. It is a large portable Philco-Trans Atlantic. Our only worry now is to keep batteries for it, but the radio section here said they would take care of that for us. We got some wire and ran a long aerial from the tent to the top of the hill behind us. Reception is really good now. It is really too nice of a radio to have here, but we will get many hours of enjoyment from it.

I had a letter from Joe Ned yesterday and as usual always appreciate his nice letters.

Today when I was on guard at the gate, a General came into the area. I really gave him a big snappy salute. You could spot his jeep a mile off as it had the lights burning and a red license plate with a star on it. All telephones start ringing when a General comes around so everyone can get shaped up.

Well Larry old buddy, guess this will have to be all for now as I'm pretty tired and its getting late. That old sack will feel good. Guess you are ready to start back to school - Ha! Write again soon.

Your brother,

Bill

P.S. Thanks for taking care of the paper for me.

Dear Mom,

Will send a few lines to you along with Larry's. There isn't anything to write that I didn't tell Larry, but wanted to let you know I dropped Ray Powell a few words the other day to let him know where I am located.

He gave me a prompt reply and said he tried two different times to call me, but had to go through too many switch boards and the distance was too great. He said send his regards to you and Dad the next time I wrote. Just wanted to let him know I was over here in this vicinity of Korea in case he happened to be in these parts some day.

I also had a nice letter from Mrs. Potts today. She said they were to leave the 18th to go see Clovis. They were to be gone about a week. Maybe it will do them good to see him. Will write more later.

Lots of Love,
Bill

Sunday Night

August 24, 1952

8:15 p.m.

Dear Mom & All,

Wrote Larry and a short note to you last night, but today received another letter from you and much to my surprise both packages came also. Have already sampled the goods and plan to put some more of it away before the night is over.

Both packages were in very good shape with the exception of the crackers being crumbled which can be expected. We managed to scrounge a box of crackers from the mess hall tonight at chow as there was some to go with the soup we had. Don't get me wrong we will also eat yours. You really sent the right can goods and I appreciate your trouble more than you know. The underwear is fine and should do me for a while. I told you before I knew the things would be in good shape as you are an old hand at wrapping packages. It really hurts me to see some of them that come through here, all due to the fact they were not properly wrapped, so I admire your art of wrapping and packing.

Along with your mail I received a very nice letter from Aunt Blanche. Like you, her letters are always so nicely written. You both could always write such an interesting letter. She got my address from Jim and Virginia.

As you have probably guessed from this letter we didn't get to make our trip I wrote about in Larry's letter due to the rain. It rained all night and has been pouring all day, and I suppose is set in for the night again. This is going to be another like we had a short time ago. If everything works out, we will try again next Sunday.

Tell Larry we listened to "Our Miss Brooks" on the radio tonight. Of course it was a re-broadcast, but really enjoyed it and also it came on the same time it did there on Sunday.

This hasn't been much, but wanted to let you know right away I received the things in good condition. It is really nice to have such a wonderful Mother to do these things for me. Thanks again!

Guess I will have to use another page after all. I have been wondering what Kenneth's plans are for school. I know it is hard to quit work

and start spending money, but by all means go on to school. My plans are to do the same and that's what I'm saving towards now.

Speaking of money, Larry seems to be doing all right for himself. He will have to get his haircuts like I do with hand clippers. Go after it old boy, but don't try to do too much.

Glad you saw the McDaniels and hope the Potts came by on their vacation and your little lunch all worked out well. I can't say enough for those two people.

I must close now as I keep thinking about the food I want to dive into. So long for this time.

Lots of Love to All,
Bill

P.S. Joe did write me about the deal he thought was coming up and from what you said he must have gotten it.

Dear Mom & All

Saturday

August 30, 1952

8:45 p.m.

Dear Mom & All,

Received your letter of the 21st today and as always welcomed the same. I would have gotten it yesterday, but was sent to "A " Battery by mistake. I also had a nice long letter front Joe Ned yesterday telling me of his new set up. Sounds like a very good deal and glad to see him get it. I can't figure out why I receive his letters in six days and it takes yours seven.

I feel badly about you saying that my mail has really been pouring in as it has been a week now since I last wrote. There really hasn't been anything to write about and each day I thought maybe I would get a letter from you so it would at least give me something to reply to.

I was very happy to hear about your wonderful time with the Potts. So glad all went off well and imagine I will get the story over again from them. If you do get the chance, sure hope you and Dad will make the trip down there some Sunday. It would sure tickle them and you will enjoy it also. They both think so much of you as the rest of the family also. I can imagine how much Clovis will appreciate your letter to him.

Speaking of the film and soup, there is no hurry on either one. From time to time, I may add a few items, but don't ever go to any trouble. What I mean is in case you do happen to be sending something this way you might throw them in. We all sure did enjoy the eats in the other package. Still have the can of peaches. We have a large metal fuse box which is used for a food locker. When any of us get anything - just pitch it in the box and everyone helps himself and share together. It is very nice working this way. I can't think of anything I need at the present for cold weather, but as I said will add a few items from time to time as the occasion may arise.

No, Dewey Ross was stationed back at 3rd Repl. Co. Thought I mentioned it to you, but guess not. However, I hear from him quite often and will send your regards which reminds me of the fact I had a letter from Earl Nagel today and he said to tell you hello.

I saw another very good movie last night. It was extraordinarily good and we all enjoyed it, "A Young Man With Ideas." I looked through the papers the package was packed with and remembered seeing it advertised as playing at the Columbia.

We now have our own shower unit in the Battery, but it won't go into operation until tomorrow. All are thrilled over this fact and consider ourselves lucky as it is to be used by the whole Battalion and all we have to do is walk down to it. Went over to the engineers yesterday and took a shower. They are located up the road about three miles. Sure hope our shower unit works out all right. All we have to worry about is keeping enough water, but with all the rain this shouldn't be any problem. It is placed in a small stream and is pumped into a tank where it is heated.

Once again in the morning myself and one of the fellows I work with plan on making our trip to Seoul. Barring no rain imagine we will make it, but at the present time it is sprinkling, so have to wait until in the morning for the final decision.

This afternoon we all got the afternoon off and had a real good softball game. After two hours of catching I was pretty well worn out. Had lots of fun though.

Well, suppose it is about time to bring this to a close as I'm running out of something to write. Sorry I went so long without writing, but don't ever worry if you go for a few days without hearing from me. This way you will know all's well and I just don't have the news to write. Tell all the people who ask about me hello and at times I find myself even thinking about some of the ones you mention. Just the other day I was thinking about Mr. McCormick and was wondering how he is making it. Clovis and I really had some good times with him and both of us went by to see him one day while I was home.

Hope all are well and not working too hard - Ha!

Lots of Love,
Bill

P.S. I'm not losing any weight and seems I am putting on a few more pounds.

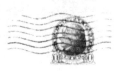

Monday Night

September 1, 1952

9:30 p.m.

Dear Mom & All,

Will take a few minutes out and try to tell you about my trip to Seoul yesterday. Really no news other than that, but thought I would write while it all is still fresh on my mind.

It was still raining a little when we left yesterday morning, but it quit before we got very far. Stayed cloudy most of the day, but didn't rain anymore. A truck load of us left around nine in the morning and arrived in Seoul about twelve thirty. Really a long old rough ride, but it was something different and was glad to get away from here for a while.

Seoul is the first place I have seen where you can actually see the destruction and poverty this war has brought to this land and its people. As I have told you before, there is nothing but hills and open fields up here where we are. I saw women yesterday for the first time in two months. Of course they were Korean, but nevertheless women.

All the large buildings are nothing but ruins as well as the whole city. It must have been reasonably modern at one time, but there isn't too much left now. The capitol building is still standing, but pretty well demolished. The streets are crowded with little children trying to give you a shoe shine or sell small trinkets which they have made. There are little shops set up all over the place. There is bound to be black marketing going on, but it is against the law to buy anything from a Korean with GI money as they call it and script to us. It is supposed to be changed into Won first by finance. You couldn't walk down the street, but a whole flock of children were following you and all they know is "you buy this." I really felt sorry for some of them. The whole city has an odor about it and when I think of this I had rather be here where at least the air is much fresher.

Now to something a little more pleasant about our trip. First of all the Army has set up a snack bar in one of the buildings there. Believe me, myself and my buddy made good use of this. I had three ham and egg sandwiches, a big dish of ice cream and later we went back for another sandwich and coffee. Did they ever taste good The ice cream

wasn't stateside as it was made from powdered milk, but even at that it tasted good.

After this we walked a good ways just looking the place over and went to the Eighth Army Theater. It was nice to see a movie indoors for a change and also sit in a seat. All we have up here is the open sky and planks. Saw "Singing In The Rain." I had missed it a time or two while around home and had always wanted to see it. We really enjoyed this.

After this we walked around a little more and was soon time to get on the truck and head back. Before leaving we drove up to one of the quarter-master outfits which have a very nice large building which sets on the top of a hill. Here Army personnel can stop off and have a free meal. We invited ourselves in and even had supper on plates and drank out of cups. Also, more ice cream and there were table clothes on the tables.

It was around six o'clock when we left and about nine when we returned here. It was right comical on the way back. You might have called us a United Nations Truck. There were soldiers hitch hiking all along the roads going back to their outfits and we picked up all we could. At one time we had ROK soldiers, which are Korean, Puerto Ricans, French, Turks and Canadian. All were speaking a different language, but so far as I was concerned they all were saying the same thing as I couldn't understand any of it.

I really enjoyed the day and food, but don't care anything about going again for a while as it is really a tiresome trip over these roads and especially in a truck. There is nothing to go back for again after you have once seen the place. I would liked to have made some pictures, but it was cloudy and I didn't have any film either. So much for all of this and hope it hasn't been too boring.

I got paid again today and they had me down for ninety bucks. All I can figure out is that my allotment didn't go to the bank. I will try to get this straightened out, but am going to hold on to the money in case they try to make up for it next month and hit me hard. I will have to begin putting some of it back anyway saving for my five day pass in Japan which is called R&R - Rest and Recuperation. This won't happen for at least another four months, but want to have a little money put back when I do get to go.

Our shower unit is now in operation and, of course, I gave it a try this afternoon. Really nice just to walk a short way rather than to ride a few miles.

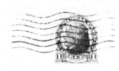
I had a nice long letter from Albert Jones yesterday and he was getting ready to head for Paducah for about twenty-seven days. If all went as planned he is probably there now and said he would be by to see you and Dad.

Well Mom this has been a pretty good letter so far as length is concerned, but don't know about the rest of it. Guess I had better sign off for now, climb the hill to our little tent and get some sack time.

Suppose Gene and Marty will be around that way about now. I haven't heard from them for about three weeks. Hope their vacation goes as planned.

Lots of Love,

Excuse all mistakes I make in my letters as I never go back over them as I think you can usually pick out what I mean.

Wednesday Night

September 3, 1952

9:30 p.m.

Dear Mom & All,

Really no news to speak of, but just wanted to let you know I received your nice letter yesterday containing the clippings of the Garrett and Sanders weddings. Also, thanks for sending Bill Smally's address and getting it for me.

I know you get tired of me writing about the rain as well as I'm tired of rain, but once again it started last night and is still at it. Along with this we got some wind from a typhoon this afternoon and cool weather with it. Actually so cool we can see our breath.

I don't know whether you mentioned or I read it in some clippings, but did get the news from somewhere about the addition to Riverside Hospital. Was pleased to hear you had such a nice time with the Throgmortons, but hated you missed the Mayfield Company.

Hope Dad's vacation comes through as planned and you can make the trip to take Kenneth to school. I suppose it is Lexington as I haven't heard otherwise, but think I mentioned to you before to let me know his plans. If Kenneth has the time, he can take time out and let me know about what's new with him and what his plans etc. are. Anyway, he will want some mail when he does get off to school so he can write me in between some of his studying. This also brings me to the fact it will add one more correspondence to your list. It hardly seems possible that four of us will be away from home, but all for a rightful purpose. Just don't wear yourself out writing letters or either start making carbon copies.

Speaking of the cake you had when the Parkers were over, sure wish I had some like it, but would be impossible to send one over here. Anyway it will he something to look forward to as well as the rest of your fine cooking. Guess this is all for now. Still doing fine and keeping busy.

Lots of Love,
Bill

Sunday Night

Sept 7, 1952

7:30 p.m.

Dear Mom & All,

This morning I had a very pleasant surprise when I received your two packages. Believe me, they really were welcomed and very tasty. We ate the small box right away and are saving the larger one to go with the can of peaches I still have you sent in your last package. The cookies, cakes or candy, a combination of all I would say were just as fresh as the day they were made. Also, they were in good shape. That must be a new recipe on me. "Number One" as the Koreans say, meaning the best.

Then this afternoon the letters from you, Gene, Martha and Larry came. I also appreciated all of them. I was beginning to wonder if it wasn't about time for Gene and Marty to be around those parts. Hope their vacation went as planned and am looking forward to hearing all about it. I know all the folks were glad to have them around for a while.

In answer to some of your questions, no, there are no Korean people around here except the Korean soldiers and a few laborers. I don't know exactly how far I am from Panmunjon, but somewhere around twenty miles. We get plenty of food and it is pretty good. Just the Army's way of fixing it as you have heard before. By no means could compare with yours. The water is all right and purified at a water point before it is brought here by trailer. That is we have a regular tank on wheels. So far as refrigeration is concerned, we get a little ice from somewhere every so often. Anything you want to know don't hesitate about asking. I don't want you worrying in the least about me as I'm safe and sound here.

Along with my other duties, I am now assistant driver for the jeep we have. I got my license yesterday. I will only drive when the regular driver is on guard or has something else to do.

This afternoon I didn't have too much work to do so I went over to see the Gates boy. My trip was useless as he had gone somewhere else for the day. Then went on down the road to try and find the other Paducah boy he had told me about, but he also was out. I found out yesterday there is a boy from Benton in our Service Battery of the 9th Field. He is

supposed to stop here someday as the fellow who told me said he would let him know I was here. Think maybe he will know Frank Nichols I worked with at the bank. It was the clerk at Service Battery who told me about this guy and said he was writing to people in Paducah, so maybe we can strike up an acquaintance.

I am enclosing the latest pictures I have made. They are not too good, but will give you a general idea of my surroundings.

Yesterday I received the UPPER ROOM and bulletin from the church. You might mention to Rev. Turner how much I appreciated it. Think I told you I wrote Bro. Turner a short time ago. Maybe he told you.

Guess this is about all for this time. Tell all hello and I will write more later. Will wait till Gene and Marty get settled again before I answer their letters. Thanks again for the cookies.

Lots of Love,
Bill

P.S. You asked what can goods I would like. Don't put yourself out and no rush, but in case you do want to send something, sometime, the potted meats of any kind always make a good snack. Also any fruit and fruit juices. No we don't have hard candy or nuts. Use your own judgment as you did well on the others.

You mentioned seeing Bro. Williams. If you run into any of them again, give them my regards.

Larry - Hello old boy, glad to get your few lines along with the rest. Seems that your team did all right and I consider second place very good. The Chiefs are also doing better than I expected. Guess you will be putting away the bats now and begin looking towards football. Keep me posted on all the games. Of course you can use the rifle, but only if Mother and Dad say so and Dad goes along with you. That is something one can't be too careful with, so always wait for Dad to be with you.

So long for now.
Bill

Friday Night

September 12, 1952

9:15 p.m.

Dear Mom & All,

Received your nice letter of the 4th today. As you found out about not receiving any mail from me for a while, as I have already told you, was due to the fact I didn't write.

Glad the storms around home didn't do any more damage than that to the wall. Hope the insurance co. takes care of it.

I knew Albert would not miss coming by to see you. He had promised me all along he would. Imagine he is having a wonderful time while on leave. He can always make himself at home no matter where he is, so glad he did just that while visiting you. He will tell me all about it.

Sure hope Joe Ned's plans worked out and he made all his connections. I know you were just as glad to have him for a short time as he was to be there. I will he looking forward to hearing of his visit if it worked out.

I don't recall the clipping of La Nelle Barron and James, but it may have slipped my mind. They will make a very nice couple and give them my regards and best wishes when seeing them again.

I almost came off my seat the other night at the movie. They had a short newscast on last year's basketball highlights and the first was Western KY. Who appears and name is mentioned, but Lynn Cole. I had forgotten about his going there and after seeing this, remembered this short being advertised in the *Sun Democrat* with him in it, but missed seeing it. At any rate thought it something to see away over here. If Kenneth has already left, mention this fact to him, as he and Lynn were pretty good friends.

Mother, I don't know if you have heard, but I got news that Billy Manley, Billy Joe Page's brother-in-law, and the boy I left with as you remember was wounded over here and is now back in the states in the hospital. I don't know how true this is, but if you can find or know anything of it, please let me know. The last I saw of him was in Japan and never did know where he went. Sure hated to hear it.

Today I made a trip after do-nuts once more for the Battalion and as usual had my share of the same. We even have a few stowed away for another day.

I had a nice letter from Bro. & Mrs. Potts yesterday, telling me about their trip and also what a good time they had with you and Dad. They think you both are really swell, but didn't have to tell me that.

This hasn't been much, but is about it for now. Guess the Florida bounders had a very nice trip.

Goodnight for now.

Lots of Love,
Bill

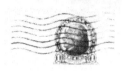

Sunday Night

September 14, 1952

7:15 p.m.

Dear Mom & All,

Just a few lines tonight to let you know I'm still around trying to dig up some news to write. Guess you get tired of me starting my so called letters this way but just like to drop in and say "hello."

There hasn't been much doing today beings it was Sunday. Missed attending church services this morning as I was on guard last night and sacked in this morning from eight until twelve. I have just come off gate guard as I was on from five until seven. We are on guard four hours during the night and pull two hours of gate guard the next day. Usually pull guard about every ten days.

It is rather cool tonight and is beginning to rain.

I may have told you about writing Bobby Nace a couple of weeks or so ago. I wasn't too surprised to receive an answer from him today, but was really surprised at the news it contained. Seems he had just become a father that morning as I suppose you have heard. He was really excited over the fact as anyone would be. Didn't say whether his wife was with him or at home.

Also another very nice letter I received today was from Mr. Murphy. He was on vacation at the time it was written and thought it so nice of him to think of me and take time out to write. As I have said before, it makes me feel so good to get a letter like his and know I have such wonderful friends thinking of me.

I haven't mentioned it before, but have been intending to tell Larry we have a dog. Not a very pretty one, but he makes all formations and is the first in chow line. Seems he takes turns about where he stays at night as he will sleep in first one tent and than another. Can also tell Larry we have just finished listening to "Our Miss Brooks." I imagine our programs are somewhat behind but we enjoy them anyway. Have already burned

out one battery, but it did pretty well as we had the radio going all the time and it lasted for three weeks. We are now playing it on army batteries so as long as we can get these, everything will be O.K.

I could never fill up another page so will say goodbye for now. Hasn't been much, but didn't have anything to write to begin with.

Lots of Love
Bill

Tuesday Night

September 16, 1952

9:30 p.m.

Dear Mom & All,

Received your nice letter and church bulletins today. I really heard the whole story of Joe Ned's visit as I also received a letter from him and the socks. Sure appreciated him doing this for me and even going to the trouble of taking wrapping material back with him. I know his visit did all of you good as it did him.

If all went as planned suppose Kenneth is now into his studies or there about at U.K. Hope all worked out well and you got to make the trip. Suppose Larry is getting down to some good old study time. It hardly seems possible the summer is over and all are returning to school.

Sure hated to hear about Louis Northington and trust it isn't as bad as they seemed to think.

As usual the same old routine with me. Last night or early this morning had quite a little storm, but I kept high, dry and comfortable here in the hex tent.

Today our PX rations came in so naturally I have been down to get my share of things, such as cigarettes, razor blades, soap and a few other odds and ends. Got some sardines, so now will have to see about getting some crackers to go with them. Also had some tomato juice which I got a can of.

Last night I saw a pretty fair movie. The first we have had in about a week as the generator has been broken down. Mickey Rooney in "Sound Off," of course an Army picture, but full of laughs as we had been through the same.

Do you remember Bob King who was home with me one Sunday. Had a letter from him yesterday. He had seen Earl Nagel, and Earl gave him my address. He even remembered you and Dad and said to tell you hello for him.

Well once again hasn't been nothing but hello and goodbye, but will have to do for now. As you have found out from my last letter, beat you to the clipping of Bobby Nace and their addi-

tion. Wonder how Ida Lou and QL feel being Grand Ma and Grand Pa. Also Mam Ma and Papa Nace are once more great-grandparents. Speaking of them, someday will get around to dropping them a few lines, but in the mean time tell them all hello.

Lots of Love,
Bill

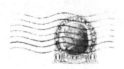

Saturday Night

September 20, 1952

10:15 p.m.

Dear Mom & All,

Just a few lines before I turn in. Had better write what little news I do have before I forget it.

Yesterday we had a very good USO show held here in our own Battery. It was the Frances Langford Show with Jon Hall, Wally Vernon and a few other entertainers. Really did us all a load of good. Outside of just the girls being there, Wally Vernon was the whole show as he is such a comedian. He plays in a lot of the comedies you see in the show. There was singing, tap dancing etc. They had their own little band with them. There were close to eight thousand soldiers over to see the show. Can you imagine that? How lucky we were it was held in our area. We went down early and got up close. I had some film and took quite a few pictures. Even got some close ups of the stars. Hope they turn out well. All you could hear was the clicking of cameras.

I also had another pleasant surprise yesterday as I received a real nice pound box of taffy candy from Lois Simmons (Martha's cousin). She sent it while she was on vacation and it took me about a month to get it. So nice of her to do this and I must write and thank her. Really hit the spot too.

Also, the paper has begun to come in. Although a month old, they are arriving in good shape and I enjoy them very much. So many little things in them I am interested to see.

The Lt. I have been working under, left for home last night and we now have a new Capt. Can't tell much about him yet, but will do as he says.

I must sign off for now and hit the sack as my candle is just about out. I could use a few candles if you have any spare ones around. In the morning is Sunday and we get about thirty minutes extra sleep. Will try to make services.

Excuse the red ink, but ran across it the other day and looked pretty good to see something besides OD. Put a little color into things. Goodbye for now.

Lots of Love,
Bill

I forgot to mention, Bill Gates, the boy from Paducah, was at the show yesterday and we made a picture together.

Also ran across a colored boy from Paducah the other day.

Tuesday Night

September 23, 1952

7:00 p.m.

Dear Mom & All,

I received your very nice long and interesting letter of the 14th. I haven't been hurting any for mail and don't ever worry about your going a few days without writing because I think you do wonderful to have so much else to do.

I also received letters from Joe Ned and one of the fellows I went through leadership school with today. I was very pleased to hear Mary Lou's husband is doing so much better.

So Kenneth finally got off to U.K. I'm sure he will make the best of it and as Joe Ned said in his letter today was very glad to see him get to go there as he has earned and worked toward it. Sorry you and Dad couldn't make the trip, but it would have been a rather tiresome one in such a short time. As you said, suppose Kenneth was all in after arriving.

It was quite funny about your mentioning Eulaine. Don't know why or anything, just before receiving your letter she happened to run through my mind and I was wondering if she was going to come home as I remembered it was just about a year ago she was there, right after I went into the Army. Thought this quite a coincidence happening this way. You had just been trying to do too much at one time, mentioning you were about to collapse. Had better watch yourself and slow down a little.

Mom, I was very inspired by the fact, you telling me what Bro. Turner said about my letter. Yes, the Lord seems to have a way of putting us where we should be at the right time. As Bro. Turner mentioned he was glad to be a member of a church that would follow me, likewise I am glad to belong to a church who doesn't forget its members no matter where they might be. It did me so much good by your telling me of this.

I know you all had a wonderful time at the park and would have liked to have been with you, but maybe this time next year the same can be repeated including Joe Ned and me. I think it was somewhere around

a year ago I received greetings from Uncle Sam, as Oct. 4th will mark my first anniversary with the U.S. Army.

Was surprised at Mr. Fleming returning to Midwest and was happy over the fact of your raise and afternoon off.

Think I mentioned in my last letter about the USO show we had with Frances Langford. What happens but I get the *Sun Democrat* of the 28th August yesterday and what do I find advertised at the Colonel Club of Paducah, but the Frances Langford Shows. Wish I had known this a few days before and would have made a special effort to see the old girl and ask about Paducah - Ha! Was quite surprising to see this after having them over here.

Yesterday, we did a little changing around here. We took down our small tent and put up a squad tent. This is much better as we have so much more room.

Last night and today I was on guard so suppose I will hit the sack early tonight. This is about all the news I can dig up for the present so had better close for now. This can't compare with the letter I received from you today, but will have to do for now.

Love to All,
Bill

P.S. Mom, if some of those, white sweat Jerseys are still around, I wouldn't mind having two or three for the cool mornings. No hurry, but if you happen to be sending something this way will appreciate your doing this. They are much better to me than the wool underwear which we are issued. Also, my comforters, which Clovis gave me last Xmas if you can find them

Saturday Night

September 27, 1952

Dear Mom, Dad & Larry,

I can now address my letters this way instead of the usual all. I meant to write a few lines last night, but since there wasn't any worth while news, thought it wasn't worth it, so today I received your nice letter along with the clippings of all the college kids and their whereabouts. Eventually guess I will get it again. While on the subject wish you would continue the paper as I enjoy it very much and of course find quite a few articles I am interested in. So far they have been arriving at the rate of two and three when I do get them which is about every three days. I will be glad to pay for it.

Was pleased to hear Kenneth got settled at U.K. and found so many friends right off. I will be looking forward to hearing from him and hope he can find time to drop a line or two my way. Does he plan on a part time job or did he say?

So you finally got your glasses. Glad you didn't put it off any longer. Imagine it will be hard to get use to them, but will pay off in the long run. I find mine quite useful in the work I'm doing. I bet it is true about you finding mistakes. You haven't said too much about your job lately. Are you still enjoying the work and find it not too hard on you? By now the newness is worn off and guess you know the set up and routine, which makes it much easier.

I didn't know Q.L. and Ida Lou had returned to Paducah. Suppose this suits them much better. How do they feel about being Grandparents?

I will agree that Friday afternoon is about one of the best times you could have off. Gives you a chance to spend all that money. If its any of my business, guess you and Dad are now getting to where you can save a little. I'm all for you and hope you can do so. Guess the grocery bill will be cut down somewhat - Ha!

As usual things are still the same with me except the weather is getting quite cool. Don't exactly care, because I know it is coming and the sooner over with the closer I will be to home. I may have told you, I now have a new Capt. to work under and today a new sergeant came in, so this so called office has undergone a complete change since I

have been here, which makes me the oldest person here in time. Not that it means anything, because the rank is what counts in the Army.

We are now listening to hit parade on the radio. Boy, the music is really good. Don't know what we would do without the radio. Have gotten many hours of enjoyment from it.

Well Mom, hardly think it worth while to start another page as there wouldn't be any thing to write, so guess I had better sign off for now. I think about you all even if I can't find more to write. Did I ever tell you I made a little frame for your picture and have it on my desk? I need one of Dad to go along with it.

Lots of Love,
Bill

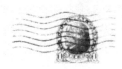

Thursday Morn.

10:15 p.m.

2 October 1952

Dear Mom, Dad & Larry,

Once again I will try to give with a few lines, I received your very nice long letter of the 22nd yesterday along with one from Kenneth, Gene & Marty. Certainly was good to hear from all.

That Kenneth may be quiet in his talking, but he certainly did write a swell letter, one of which I enjoyed very much. He seems to be well satisfied thus far. I will answer it right away as imagine he likes mail also. I would have done a little letter writing last night, but was on guard and that explains my writing of this hour of the day. I have to go on again at eleven which won't give me much time on this letter.

From the way you described the weather at home, it must be about the same as we are having. Soon as the sun goes down it becomes quite cool, but the days are still pleasantly warm.

Gene & Marty also wrote a nice long letter telling me of their wonderful vacation. They even sent some of the pictures along. I will send them all back with the exception of one where they are together beings I don't have a picture of either of them. Sounded as if they both had plenty of work waiting for them, but that was to be expected.

Did I tell you my watch went bad on me. Can't complain as it has been a good one no more than I paid for it and as long as I've had it. Suppose it can be fixed all right – just gains quite a bit of time. I plan on sending it home, but there is no need in having it fixed as it would probably take too long. So, since this happened the other day when PX rations came in, what do we get but a Baby Ben alarm clock I was the first to latch on to it and now wake up by an alarm. Suppose you have seen them. It cost only four dollars and figured it worth that since my watch was on the "blink." So small I can carry it around with me and leave it setting on my desk.

Quite a few of the guys have them to wake up with.

We also managed to get enough lumber to build a small frame around the tent where we work. They are working on it today, but as

I told you I'm on guard and can't help out. Should make it a little warmer this winter.

Mom, I wish there was more to write about, but don't know what it would be. It is about time for me to go on guard so guess I had better close for now. Give my regards to all and I will write again soon.

Lots of Love,
Bill

P.S. Excuse this long paper, just happened to have it handy.

Monday Night

October 6, 1952

9:00 p.m.

Dear Mom, Dad & Larry,

Was glad to receive your letter of the 27th today, and seems like the mail is coming your way also. You know there is no one we had rather write to than our Mother.

Your letter carried the first news of the Travis baby. I'm sure I will hear from them in the near future. Would appreciate very much you sending some little something for us. Very nice of them to remember you in their announcements.

Yes, I found out yesterday Jimmy Hill is on his way home as I had a visitor from Paducah. It was the Gibson boy I spoke of from Lone Oak. He came over and we had a real nice time talking about the old town and he told me about Jimmy Hill as he had seen him not too long ago. I didn't know the Gibson boy, but it doesn't take long to get acquainted with someone from your home town over here. He also entered the Army with Joe Ned and he knew him. Looks like before I get out of this Army, will run into all the boys Joe left with somewhere or the other. This makes a total of five. Three over here and two while at Breckinridge.

Hope the trip to St. Louis turned out as planned and everyone had a good time. I know Larry & Dickie went all out for this. We have been getting rebroadcasts of the World Series. Guess Larry kept up with all these events.

You would never guess what we have been doing the last couple nights and one reason for my not writing sooner. We have been having some hot games of ping pong. The table is not quite as large as standard size as its nothing more than a sheet of plywood we picked up. Got the paddles and balls down from Special Services. Our biggest problem was a net, but we put some string across the middle and it worked out pretty well. Had a good time anyway.

We got a stove for our tent today, but haven't put it up yet. Suppose we will get to it tomorrow. Later on we are supposed to get another. Could sure use a little heat some of these mornings, but warms up on up in the day.

Seems as each time I write my letters get shorter, but sometimes there is no news worth writing and then again can dig up some kind of ramblings.

I might mention the fact I attended church services yesterday morning and as usual had a nice little worship service. Had a different Chaplain as ours is on R and R to Japan.

Well Mom, this finds me without anymore to say for the present so will sign off and crawl into a good warm sleeping bag. It is amazing how warm they are. They are lined with feathers.

Don't any of you work too hard and tell all hello.

Lots of Love,
Bill

Tuesday

12:00 p.m.

14 October 1952

Dear Mom, Dad & Larry,

Seems that it has now been a week since I last wrote. Have been trying to dash off a few lines every night, but have been keeping busy and always ready to hit the sack quick as possible. Also have been working some at night trying to get caught up with some work. Don't ever begin to worry if you go a week or a little longer without hearing from me. You will know its just that there has been nothing to write about.

I received your very nice long letter of the 3rd yesterday and as I have already told you that date did ring a bell in my memory.

Was glad to hear you had such a wonderful trip to St. Louis. I know all had a swell time and certainly deserved it

About the only news with me is that I took Sunday off and headed back towards Seoul once more. This is one reason I have so much work piled up on me. However, I didn't make it on into the City of Seoul as I decided to get off the truck about three miles outside of Seoul and go over to the 3rd Replacement Co. and see Dewey Ross as I hadn't seen him since we got here. He was really glad I came over and another very good friend of ours who went through basic with us is now there and he had run across. We went over to see him and all had a nice afternoon together.

I had to take time out to go to chow and it is now around 1:00 o'clock. Don't know if I will get this finished before tonight or not.

Back to my trip Sunday. When I came into Korea they were just setting the rice out and Sunday they were cutting it. The rice patties were right pretty as they were a golden yellow. The day was rather cool, but made the trip all right.

I had a letter from Omar Willis the other day and he told me all about his five days in Japan. I am really looking forward to mine which should come in the middle of winter. Rather a bad time to go, but will enjoy it just the same.

Also, I had a letter from the Potts yesterday, Clovis was home for about four days and carried his car back to camp with him. Said they

were planning on going to Paducah in a few days, so imagine they contacted you, if they got to go.

I have guard duty again tonight so that is one reason I'm taking a few minutes now to write. I will try not to go so long next time.

The papers are still coming through and I enjoy looking through them and finding changes of Paducah.

Mom, this hasn't been much of a letter, but thought I had at least better say hello before another day passes. Don't worry about me getting cold as we now have our little stove and plenty of clothing.

I must close for now and do a little typing. Will write more in a day or so.

Lots of Love,
Bill

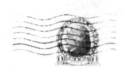

Saturday

18 October 1952

12:00 p.m.

Dear Mom, Dad & Larry,

Think it is time once more to send my few lines your way. At any rate wanted to let you know if you don't hear from me for a while it is because we are moving, which is supposed to come in the next few days. Imagine the mail might be delayed, but will write soon as we get settled once more. Don't know where we are headed, but will tell you more when we get there.

I had quite a surprise the other day when I was looking through the little paper we get called "Stars & Stripes" which is printed in Japan by the Armed Forces and we get a week later. What do I find, but a picture of Gloria Stice and her being named "Cotton Queen." It was almost like a letter to see a picture of someone I knew and the home town name in such a paper. Not only this, but think I told you about a friend of Bob Wolff's wife in Iowa who writes to me occasionally. She sends the same picture which was in their paper and wanted to know if I knew the girl. It was probably plastered all over the *Sun Democrat*. The guys around here didn't want to believe I knew the girl and had dated her some while in High School. That picture sure got around the country.

Another pleasant surprise I had was a very nice card from the Jr. Dept. of the church and signed by all the members of my former Sunday School Class. I really did appreciate this and it meant a whole lot to me. I will try to write them a note later on, but express my appreciation to them, and Mrs. Russell and Mrs. Lovvo. Think I remember you saying you would have some of them in your class.

This is about all the news I can dig up for the present time. The weather is still getting cooler and we have had ice a couple of mornings. Everything is beginning to look like winter. Think I mentioned how beautiful the hills are now in all their colors. Would look much prettier somewhere besides Korea.

This about covers the latest events with me. Wish I could write more, but thought I had better get this little bit on the way. I will write more soon as I hear from you.

Hope you can read this as I'm sitting on my bunk and writing on a box. Trust all is well with you and everything at home is going well.

Lots of Love,
Bill

26 October 1952

Sunday 1:30 p.m.

Dear Dad,

Yesterday I received the very nice card which Mom sent. I appreciated the card very much, but was even more glad to get the news which it contained of you being elected to the Board of Stewards. I considered it a great honor myself and sure you do also. It is something we both can be proud of as well as our family. Like Mother said, she is proud of the fact she has seen her father, husband and son, all Stewards in The Methodist Church. Let me take this opportunity to congratulate you on being named a Steward in Fountain Avenue Methodist Church.

Not only did I receive the card yesterday, but along with it came the package of eats. I really did appreciate them and we are making good use of the same. You will never know how it makes me feel to have such wonderful parents, who always put their children first and never forget them when they are away. I hope to be able to show all my appreciation someday.

I had a letter from Kenneth yesterday also and enjoy hearing from him. Glad he is doing so well, but as he says things are pretty rough.

I went to Church Services this morning and as usual enjoyed them very much. Although the Chaplain is a colored fellow, he is very nice and is doing good work. I have had the chance to talk with him quite a few times as he drops around here quite often.

We are about to get straightened out once more after our move. We got our stove up today so of course we will try it out tonight. This morning the weather was down to about 25 degrees above. We are fortunate in having a hex tent as they are about the warmest and will be even better with a stove. Really a nice little heater.

I don't think I mentioned it, but directly in front of us is a very large mountain peak. It is really beautiful when the sun goes down as it turns a dark purple from the shadows.

Well Dad, once again I will say it means a whole lot to me for you being named a Steward. Take care of yourself and don't work too hard.

Lots of Love,
Bill

Friday Night

Oct 31, 1952

Dear Mom,

Received your very nice long letter of the 21st today. It really carried the news. Also a couple of days ago I received the box of cookies. They really were good and all the boys bragged on them and wanted to know if my Mother made them. Thanks very much. They were appreciated both by me and the rest.

Along with your letter today came one from Joe, but wasn't happy over the news it contained. It was just as much of a shock to me as it was to him I'm sure. I will write him a letter and address it to home. As much as I hate to see him come over, no more time than he has, it will pass very fast. It will probably hurt you somewhat to see us both over this way, but don't worry as all will be fine.

Today has been another one of those rainy ones in Korea. Turned warm last night and we were sure of the rain as that's the way it comes. Now after a day of rain it is turning somewhat colder.

We got the floor back in our tent yesterday and finished putting up the frame today. Had to cut the floor into sections after we got the word to move, but fitted back together rather well.

So you now have a desk of your own. Really getting to be a big shot now. Just kidding, glad you have more room and find working easier.

I haven't been able to find out exactly where Omar Willis is located. Haven't been out of the area since being here. I was glad to get the news of Mr. Willis joining the church. Give him my congratulations. He will find it a great benefit and blessing.

I don't recall ever knowing W.B. Batts. I wouldn't know where to begin looking for him without an address.

When talking about your drive and all the beautiful country it even ran through my mind about my trip to Meade and then you went on to mention it. As I told you before the mountains and hills over here were really beautiful a few weeks ago.

Do hope Mama Nace is doing better and she wasn't sick too long. Give them my regards and hope she is up once again.

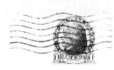

This isn't what I like to call a letter, but about all I can do for now. Want to write Joe a few lines, so maybe I can think of more in the meantime. Tell Larry not to get married on all that money he is making. Bet he is beginning to think about dating anyway. How about it?

Lots of Love,
Bill

William H. Nace

Monday Night

November 3, 1952

6:45 p.m.

Dear Mom & All,

Received your nice long letter of the 26th today. As I always say, glad to hear from you as your letters are so interesting and contain the news I like to hear.

There still isn't any news worth writing except that I did contact Omar Willis yesterday. Don't mean I saw him, but got through to him on the phone as we have a power phone here and thought I would give it a try. Had no trouble hearing him and we had a nice conversation. I went to our message center and got the code names of outfits and switchboards to go through. I told him about Joe's orders and naturally he was surprised at hearing such news. The best we could figure out, we are not too far from each other and he said he would stop by, if ever over this way.

Suppose Joe is enjoying his stay at home. It is really hard to enjoy yourself knowing it won't be long and the place you are headed. Hate to see him headed this way, but will give anything to see him. Sure hope things work out where we can get together.

I was very much surprised to hear about the phone call you had from the nice young lady you spoke of. I can't imagine what you talked about so long. I was still under the impression she was engaged, but Albert Jones told me different in a letter I received from him. So far I haven't heard from her.

I know all of you enjoyed the trip up to see the Macks and am sure it was a treat both to Aunt Leetha & Uncle Morrell as it was to the Macks.

I went to church services yesterday morning. We had a nice little group and all enjoyed the services. We even have a few Korean Soldiers to attend and it does me good to see this.

I just can't seem to write a letter anymore. There is no news as its the same old thing over and over. I haven't been out of the area since getting here. Don't ever say you will try to do better next time in your letters. Wish I could keep up with them.

125

Might add I received some pictures from Bob Wolff's wife which were made when we were in KY, and will send them home.

Guess I had better sign off for now.

Lots of Love,
Bill

Fountain Avenue Methodist Church

300 Fountain Avenue

Paducah, Kentucky

BEDFORD TURNER, D.D.
MINISTER
RESIDENCE PHONE 3-1031

MRS. J. W. JOHNSON
CHURCH SECRETARY
OFFICE PHONE 3-0005

November 14, 1952

Dear Bill:

Your good letter came today, and your message
is so fine— just like you always do everything.

Your church grows at the rate of three each
Sunday. Services are well attended. Vespers at
5 p.m. will begin November 30. Our M. Y. F. groups
have an attendance of more than seventy with refresh-
ments. We sure do miss you.

Your Dad is on our Board of Stewards and I am
happy about it.

Love and best wishes, I am

Faithfully,

Bedford Turner

Hello Bill:

Thought you might like to know that your group has
started a class in the balcony, Valerie is the teacher and
they have a nice bunch every Sunday morning. Don't think
they have named the class yet but it is for the young adults
who are single.

The MYF had a nice letter from Jimmy Rice and we had
one from Jimmy Cromwell. By the way my brother is in Germany
right over next to the Russian border.

The UEM starts Sunday, this will be headquarters for
the preachers all over the district. The women of the church
will give them their lunch every day and they are also fixing
supper for the laymen who go out to visit every evening. That
kitchen will realy be hummin'.

Hope the preacher didn't mind my adding a postscript.
Just thought you might like to hear some of the details.

Yours truly,

12 November 1952

Wednesday Night

7:30 p.m.

Dear Mom & All,

Guess I had better take time out to drop you a few lines as it has now been close to a week since I last wrote. Each day I have been thinking I would receive a letter from you, but the mail is all fouled up. I know it isn't because you haven't been writing as I haven't received any mail in almost a week. Guess it will all come in due time and once more I will be behind in my correspondence.

By the time you receive this suppose Joe Ned will be on his way. I haven't heard as yet about his getting home as the last letter I had you were expecting him that night. Hope the news didn't go too hard with you, but no one knows better than you, that all is well as long as we keep faith in the Lord and do His will. I know you enjoyed having him and all had a nice time while he was at home.

The weather has become quite cold and believe it or not we had our first snow the other morning. Didn't last long as the sun came out and melted it all. We are keeping plenty warm as our stove really heats the small tent in which we sleep.

Of course we were all interested in the outcome of the election. Time will only prove the results. I think Ike really went over more than what most people expected.

Don't think I mentioned to you, but you may already know I received a letter the other day from the M.Y.F. Each member there that night added a line or so, and I really did appreciate this. It really meant a whole lot to me in their thinking of me and to write such a letter. I have already replied, telling them how much I appreciated this.

Last Saturday we had another Court Martial Case to come up, and once more I was the reporter, so I have been tied up with that for the past few days. This is one big job as so many papers have to be filled out and a record of the trial made. I am beginning to think I am really essential to the organization as typists are hard to find and everyone comes to me.

I must close for now and go get some chow. Tell all hello and I will write soon as possible. It is rumored we are going over towards where Omar Willis is located. Will try to contact him if this is so.

Lots of Love,
Bill

7.30 p.m.

P.S. I didn't seal my letter thinking maybe I would hear from you when the mail came in and sure enough there was a letter of the 8th.

I don't blame Larry for quitting his paper route or as you say by Dad's request. The weather will be cold now and really isn't worth it.

Also in today's mail I had a letter from Albert Jones. Believe it or not, that boy wrote fourteen pages telling me all about Paducah and what he did while there. It was just like reading a book.

I forgot to mention I also had a very nice letter from Jimmy Hough the other day. Another I will try to answer soon.

Hope the furnace is fixed up and operating by now. I was surprised at it being so cool there this time of the year.

Guess this is about all for now. Thanks for the page from the "Courier Journal."

On lookout, north of the 38th parallel.

Sunday Night

November 16, 1952

8:00 p.m.

Dear Mom & All,

Received your letter of the 2nd a few days ago and sorry about not answering it sooner. I fixed up the pictures to mail last night and really meant to write a few lines, but was so tired due to the fact I had guard the night before, decided to wait until tonight. I waited so long about answering along comes your letter of the 7th today, plus the box containing the sweat shirts, one of which I have on now, the candles, loafer socks and peanut brittle. The box was in perfect shape as they all always are. Thanks a million for the trouble.

Not only did I receive your box today, but much to my surprise I get a box of cookies from the Willing Workers S.S. Class of the church. It certainly was a nice box and fixed up so well. They were all packed in a tin box, which contained about six layers of different kind of cookies. This did me so much good that they would think of me in such a way as this. The first thing I did tonight was write a thank you note to the class, but if you happen to see any of them or the president of the class, you, too, could tell them how much I appreciated this.

I had a letter from Martha and Gene the other day and they told me about their trip to Paducah. I know you enjoyed having them as well as Joe Ned. Suppose Joe had a wonderful time while home and now on his way to Seattle. Guess he will keep me informed as to his moving along with you. Hope everything works out well for him as I rather imagine he might have been a little more downhearted than I was. Do hope his trip to Lexington came off as planned and he got to see Kenneth. Also the trip to Bloomington. I know Gene and Martha were planning on it as they mentioned it to me in their letter.

The weather continues to be cool here and we had a little sleet this afternoon. Tell Larry we have what is known as "Mickey Mouse Boots" issued to us yesterday. They are supposed to be the real thing for keeping your feet warm. The name fits well as that's what they look like. They are all rubber with some kind of packing and lace just like a regular boot.

This would be the real thing for Dad when he is out. Mine fit perfect, but as yet haven't worn them. Will have to do so before too long.

This morning I attended church services and as usual enjoyed it very much. We continue to have good crowds and find them a great benefit and blessing to us all.

This M/Sgt Dowdy in some of the pictures I sent is now HQ's Battery 1st Sgt. He was Sgt. Major of the Battalion and who I worked under. He is really a nice guy and has been in the Army for 25 years. He got his retirement after getting over here and was then called back for two more years. The reason I'm telling you this is due to the fact he is trying to get me as his clerk of Headquarters Battery as the one there is due to rotate in January. I don't know if it will work out, but would really like to have the job. The only trouble is turning me loose here. The job I have now is in Headquarters Battery, but in the S1 Section for the Battalion. Think I would have it somewhat easier if I could make the change.

You can tell Larry not to look for this anytime soon, but a week or so ago we had a mobile PX come into the area where you could place orders for Christmas gifts through the Main Central Exchange of Japan. I ordered him a jacket which will he too large I'm sure, but he can keep it until he grows into it, or more or less as a souvenir. They didn't have a very large assortment so I didn't think it worth while to order anything for you and Dad. Another thing you weren't sure to get what you ordered as they sometimes have to substitute. I will try to send you something while on R&R.

Maybe I told you. I should be going on R&R next month if things work out. This would be a fine Christmas present for me.

Guess this is about enough for this time as I have about covered everything of any interest. Hope all are well and not working too hard.

Lots of Love,
Bill

P.S. I received the clippings of Gloria Stice and convinced everyone. Your letter which was mailed at the same time was a day later getting here as it was mis-sorted. Don't mind me telling you, but think it was due to the fact you have been addressing the last few Headquarters Btry, 3rd Infantry Division and should be Headquarters Btry, 9th FA Bn. You have put all the address on it, but this particular letter went to Headquarters of the 3rd Infantry Division first. Just to prevent this from happening again thought I would mention it.

Sunday Night

23 November 1952

7:30 p.m.

Dear Mom & All,

Guess it is about time I drop a few lines your way once more. Nothing new as usual, but maybe I can ramble off something.

I didn't make church services this morning as I was on guard last night. They plan on having a Thanksgiving Service Thursday, so I will attend them.

Yesterday I received a letter from Omar Willis stating they had moved and the best I could tell he is somewhere around the place I was before. Seems that we will never get around to seeing each other. Although we were never real close friends, I appreciate his keeping in contact with me.

Also in yesterday's mail I received a very nice note from Rev. Turner and Mildred Johnson. I am going to enclose it with this letter as I would like to keep it. You may tell Mildred Johnson how much I appreciated her few lines.

Some more mail which I received since last writing was a very nice box of eats from a little girl who isn't too far away from you, namely on Palm Street. Sure surprised me in getting this, but sure did appreciate it.

I might also add that I have received a letter from Mrs. Potts and Virginia Travis. She told me all about the baby and how much she appreciated the gift you sent for us both. I know it meant a lot to her from what she said. I must answer all these letters, but as I always say, I put you first.

Suppose Joe Ned is about ready for his trip if he hasn't already started. I expect to be hearing from him before too long. I wrote Albert sometime ago telling him Joe would be out that way. Sure hope they can get together and visit the Travises. While talking about Joe, I also received his letter this week written while he was home. The same day I got one from Kenneth and they both told me what a wonderful time they had at homecoming. I answered Kenneth's letter on the 21st and wished him a Happy Birthday although late as it might be.

Seems that all I have done is tell you about my mail this week, but that's about all the news I have. I will close now and write again soon.

Lots of Love
Bill

Thanksgiving

November 27, 1952

1:30 p.m.

Dear Mom, Dad, and Larry,

Yes, it is Thanksgiving Day in Korea and I have just finished a very fine Dinner. Today is rather quite, so thought this the perfect time to answer your nice long letter of 16, which I received yesterday.

We had a very nice church service this morning and one which meant a whole lot to me. There was a good crowd and everyone seemed to enjoy it so much. We were even given a bulletin which I will enclose in this letter.

We had the regular traditional Army dinner as well as could be prepared here. Would have been much better if we could have eaten from plates instead of mess gears, but all were thankful for what we did have as we are so much more fortunate than so many others. Our meal consisted of Turkey, dressing, green peas, gravy, shrimp salad, potatoes, bread, pumpkin pie, fruit cake, ice cream, nuts, gum drops, olives, celery, cranberry sauce and coffee, so you can readily see we had a mess gear full. There is no need to say that no matter how much we had or how it was prepared, none of it could take the place of your meals and cooking.

Do hope Kenneth got home for the holiday and also Gene and Martha. I know you had a very nice Thanksgiving and so far mine has been wonderful, but one I shall never forget, I am reminded that last Thanksgiving I spent on K.P. so don't know but what this one was even better, though in Korea. So much for my day and on to something else.

Don't think I mentioned in my last letter, but I received my election ballot from the Court House of Paducah, Kentucky. Just a little late don't you think? It was mailed on the 18th of October and was over a month receiving it.

I was glad to hear Jimmy and Ginny had made it down to spend the weekend with Martha and Gene. Sorry you missed seeing them. I don't believe Joe has ever met Ginny, so I am in hopes he got to contact them while in Chicago. I haven't heard from Joe as yet, but should be receiving a letter soon. I have just been wondering, how and where Joe spent today.

You spoke of locating my exact whereabouts on the map from Newsweek. We had that same map around here as someone cut it out of Newsweek. I am sure you were pretty much right about the spot you picked as it was very plain on it.

Imagine the Taylors are enjoying their new Studebaker. You never can tell Dad might accidentally have a new car by the time I get home for me to run around in - Ha! Whether he does or not, this is one of the first things I plan on doing is buying a new car. I plan on having somewhere around enough to pay cash for it. I was glad you checked on my allotment, as this is one of the things I have been meaning to tell you to do. If it isn't too much trouble, wish you would check my balance and let me know what it is. Isn't it about time for my insurance to be due? Whatever it is, go right ahead and write a check for it. You know to do this anytime.

You can imagine how surprised I was to read Bobbye Stivers Article. From what she wrote, my letter must have really been appreciated. I never did get a letter from her, but guess this was the reply. I will return the clipping, as I too would like to keep it.

Seems that I have done a pretty good job of writing a letter for a change. Think I have about covered everything so see no need of rambling on. Hope all are well. I might add about the weather this Thanksgiving Day. It isn't cold, but has been raining most of the day and is at it once more.

Lots of Love,
Bill

William H. Nace

Sunday Night

November 30, 1952

730 p.m.

Dear Dad,

The other day I received one of the most appreciated letters I have gotten while over here. This letter as you know was from none other than yourself. It meant so much to me that you sat down and wrote such a letter. Wish you would do this more often or at least when you can find the time.

Your letter, Mom's Thanksgiving Card and two packages all arrived the day after Thanksgiving. Really appreciated all of them more arriving on this day as we had so much on Thanksgiving. After all, it was Thanksgiving at home. The cookies arrived in perfect shape and everyone really did brag on them. We made hot chocolate and had the cookies.

Went very good together. Don't bother to send anymore hot chocolate by airmail as I noticed how much it cost, Really hits the spot, but not for that price.

Dad, I am so glad you now have a little time to work with the church. Not that you never did want to, but as I say now have a little extra time to get out and do this work. Wish I was there to also help.

I am all for Larry having the shot gun, but this is one thing you cannot be too careful about. Will do you both good to get out and do a little hunting.

Do hope your raise came through, because every little bit counts. I want to see you and Mom get a little ahead now and maybe be thinking about a house when I get home. I am trying to save every penny, I can while over here.

Today has been cloudy and rather cold. This afternoon the Third Division Band came up and gave a short concert. Really did enjoy the music. Reminded me of real football weather with the band.

Also, today was payday. Only drew thirty-six dollars, but nothing to spend that on. As I said before, saving it for R&R.

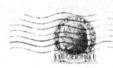

This hasn't been much of a letter, but Dad I really did appreciate such a very nice letter from you. It did me so much good. I have started receiving the *Sun Democrat* once more.

Love to all,
Bill

William H. Nace

November 30, 1952

9:00 p.m.

Dear Larry:

Just wanted you to know I didn't forget your "Birthday." Wish I could celebrate with you. All I can do is wish you "Happy birthday and many happy returns to a swell brother." Will send you something when I go to Japan on R&R.

As Ever,
Bill

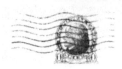

 HEADQUARTERS BATTERY
9th FIELD ARTILLERY BATTALION
3rd INFANTRY DIVISION
KOREA

November 30, 1952
9:00 P.M.

DEAR LARRY:
Just wanted you to know I didn't forget your "Birthday." Wish I could celebrate with you. All I can do is wish you. ——

"HAPPY BIRTHDAY"
AND
MANY HAPPY RETURNS
to

A SWELL BROTHER

Will SEND you something when I go to Japan on R&R.

AS EVER,

Bill

Tuesday Night

7:30 p.m.

2 December 1952

Dear Mom & All,

Received your nice letter of the 23rd today. As always I am glad to receive such nice long letters from you. The mail is about a couple of days behind what it ordinary is. Suppose this is due to the Christmas mail which is starting to pour in.

Yesterday it rained all day and began to get cold around dark. Of course this turned the rain into snow and this morning we had about four inches of the same. Tonight is the coldest we have had. Someone said the latest report was 10 degrees. It sure feels like it here in the tent. Myself and three of the other guys are all around the stove writing letters.

Since you mentioned my stationery as you can see I am now out. It was bought from unit funds. Someone sent back to the States and had it printed. You can see what I'm using for stationery now, but I can at least keep my lines straight.

As I mentioned in Dad's letter, I think it all right for Larry to have the gun. Maybe I won't have to buy one now - can use his. Just teach him all the safety precautions of having and using it.

So far, I still haven't heard from Joe Ned. Can't understand this as you have already heard and then wrote me. Guess I will be receiving word from him before too long. Was so glad he got to visit with Aunt Blanche and family when he was in Chicago.

I had a letter from Virginia Travis yesterday, but she didn't say anything about Joe. Don't suppose she even knew he was out their way. As I have said before, they sure are swell people. Said she was just thinking about me and would write a few lines.

I might add I received a very nice letter from Bobbye Stivers yesterday. Was very glad to get such a letter. She told me all about your lengthy conversation and went on to say she sure thought you a sweet person and enjoyed talking to you. Of course she didn't have to tell me this as I already have known this for a long time. Appreciated her saying this. I will almost be afraid to come home with you and Dad keep-

ing my girls lined up for me. After all though, guess someone has to keep them in line while I'm so far away - Ha!

Also received a letter front Ernest Walls yesterday. Was very glad to hear from him as this was the first letter he has written in sometime. Wants me to think about coming back to the bank, but suppose I will be the "College Kid."

Forgot to mention while on the subject of B. Stivers. I am now receiving the S.D. once more. The first edition I received carried the news of the murder. Was really shocked when reading this. I knew the Wurth boy, or at least think it was the same one. I noticed the paper left the girl's name out – was just wondering if you knew who was with him.

Well, I suppose I had better bring this to a close and write a few of these women - Ha! Notice I put you first - before any of them, at least until I find the right one which isn't yet. Hope all are well.

Lots of Love,
Bill

Tuesday Night

9 December 1952

8:00 p.m.

Dear Mom & All,

Received your letter of the 29th today and can't even remember the last letter I wrote to you. The time is going by so fast I can't keep up with it or the last time I wrote. Whenever you go a while without hearing, don't ever worry as you can rest assured I am safe and sound, just no news to write or the time to do it after I get through with everything else. So many people are so nice to write I try to keep up with my correspondence and answer them when I get a letter.

I was very excited about the clipping as I knew it was going to be about the Thanksgiving Day football game. Expected to see Tilghman by a big score and you can imagine what a big let down when I opened it up. Such things keep up the rivalry between the two schools and sometime work out for the best although we hate to see our team beat.

Was very sorry to read the clipping about the Stewart baby. I know this was a great shock to everyone as only a short time ago they were rejoicing over the new arrival.

Most of our snow is gone now, but here you never can tell when more will come. The hills are all still covered with snow and today I think the most beautiful sunset I have ever seen appeared. Over behind all the snow covered mountains was a gorgeous mixture of pink and blue over the white. I had to just stop and thank the Lord for such beautiful picturesque scenes in such a place like this.

Seems that Joe did as well in Seattle as I did. I received letters from him, Albert and the Travises all the same day telling me what a wonderful time all had. Between the three of them I got the whole story. All mentioned about Albert calling Lee, telling them he had someone they would like to see. When he and Virginia came down to pick them up, both Lee and Virginia - first seeing Joe thought it was me. I wrote Lee and Virginia thanking them for showing Joe such a good time. I know how much it meant to me.

I am still waiting to receive word from Joe Ned as to his whereabouts. He should be arriving over this way by this time. I am still in

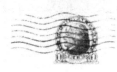

hopes he will stay in Japan. Doesn't look now as if I will get my five day leave to Japan until Spring. There isn't anyone who can take my place while I go. Makes me sound pretty important, but not everyone can do this work.

I received a letter from Kenneth today and he was telling me about his weekend at home. As he said, there wouldn't be any need of me answering that letter as he would be home for the Xmas holidays soon. Guess he will be there by the time you receive this.

Well Mom, this hasn't been much of a letter as usual, Suppose everyone at home is getting a little Xmas spirit including all the rush etc. In case I don't get another letter to you before Xmas, I will say, "Merry Christmas" to all and may God Bless You.

Lots of Love,
Bill

Monday Night

December 15, 1952

8:30 p.m.

Dear Mom & All,

Received your letter of the 3rd a few days ago and sorry I haven't answered sooner, but really haven't had the time. We have really been keeping busy and I'm away behind in my correspondence.

Was sure sorry to get the word of Earl Nagel. He had been owing me a letter and I was beginning to wonder what had happened to him. I won't write until I receive a letter from him to get his address. Certainly was a nice letter his girl wrote and I appreciated you sending it.

Believe it or not - we have a Christmas tree although it is only eighteen inches high and artificial. The Sgt's wife sent the tree to him and it is really cute. We even got to decorate it as the tree opened up and all the decorations were enclosed to go on it. We had quite the time and don't know when I have enjoyed decorating a tree more.

Not only this, but the same Sgt. received news that same day that he had become a father. Eight pound boy which was born on 7 December. He was one happy guy. Had the cigars and all.

I had quite a bit of Christmas today as I received four packages. Betty & Otley sent me the nicest box of home made candy. It is really good and I sure appreciated their doing this. Along with theirs came one from Gene and Marty. A lot of can goods, chewing gum and two sweat jerseys, plus three big red candles which we are going to place on the box with our tree. Sue Habacker sent me a large box of eats and Nancy Reaves from Dyersburg sent a box of candy and a carton of cigarettes. Gosh, we will be eating for the rest of the time I'm here. Of course the rest are receiving packages also, so you can bet we won't go hungry for a while. A11 the packages were wrapped very nicely and in Christmas paper besides, so made me more or less get the Christmas Spirit.

I think your stationery is very nice and the way you are writing letters at the present time, I will agree you certainly need it.

Sure was glad Kenneth made it home, but I was sure he would. I know you were glad to have him. Speaking of him being so big, don't

know if I have mentioned, but I sometimes wonder just how much I now weigh. I have really put on the weight since being over here.

More mail I have received is from Gary, Ind. Had a real long nice letter from Virginia and Jimmy telling me what they had been doing and how much they enjoyed Joe's short visit. Then a day or two later who do I receive a letter from but Ruth Ann. Thought it mighty sweet of her to write me and appreciated her letter. Will try to drop her a few lines soon. Oh! yes, suppose Dad will be interested to know I received a letter from Wanda - Ha!

Mom, this hasn't been much, but about all I can do for now. Hope all are well and I will try to write more soon.

Lots of Love,
Bill

Keeping warm during the infamous Korean winters.

William H. Nace

Friday Night

December 19, 1952

8:00 p.m.

Dear Mom & All,

Received your letter of the 11th today and as always glad to receive news from home. You can bet your letters do as much good here as you say mine do there.

Once again this morning we woke up to find the ground covered with snow and continued snowing for a few hours this morning. Guess this will be the way it will be for the rest of the winter, practically get rid of one snow and along comes another.

Like you, I still haven't heard from Joe Ned, although I received a change of address card from him today, only giving his Provision Co. There is no need in me writing to this address as he will hear faster by my waiting until I get a direct address.

While on the subject of Joe, I was very glad to get the name of his friend Don Karlberg who is in the 3rd Signal Co. and also located in this vicinity. Only had to go through one switchboard to locate him, so I gave it a try and had no trouble. It just so happens, this fellow has been over here for eleven months. He was with Joe at Camp Gordon and was wondering what had become of him. He was very glad I called and is trying to come over tomorrow. Said he would sure like to meet me and could find out where Joe is located through me. Will let you know if he comes over.

Also in today's mail, I was very much surprised to receive a box of candy and some candles from the Hannins. Really appreciated their doing this.

I have already written them a thank you note. Mom, it has really done me good to receive so many cards and packages from people I never would have thought about doing such things. Yesterday I received a Xmas Card and short note from Bill and Joe Whedon, just such people as this which I know must be thinking of me. Of course you might know about most of these as I suppose it is you who passes out my address. I am going to keep all my Xmas Cards and send them home as you will probably want to see them. While on the subject of Xmas Cards,

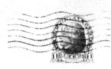

I also received yours today and it contained a very inspiring message which meant a whole lot to me - Thanks!

There really isn't anything worth writing as usual, but can always tell you about my mail as that's about all I ever I do. Yes, I know Margaret House you spoke of - if I remember correctly she is engaged. Always give anyone that asks about me my regards. Better close for now.

Love to All,

Bill

William H. Nace

Thursday Night

25 December 1952

Dear Mom & All,

This will be a day I shall always remember when Christmas rolls around. The Christmas I spent in Korea. All in all, has been a nice day, but would have never known it was Christmas without the nice dinner we had.

Although here at this time I consider myself so much more fortunate than others and don't know but what Christmas has meant more to me than it ever did before, as far as true meaning goes.

Last night several of the boys got together here in our tent and we all put out things to eat which we had received in the mail, nuts, candy, fruit cake, etc. There was even one colored boy in the bunch. He had a great big fruit cake which he brought over. This was really inspiring to me in someway, by all of us just sitting here on Christmas Eve sharing what we had with each other. We have been eating like mad around here for the past two or three weeks and still have plenty left. The latest package I received was a three pound box of chocolates from Aunt Blanch and Uncle James. Really is a nice box and I appreciated it very much. Will have to write them a short letter thanking them for the same.

This morning the Chaplain held Christmas Services and everyone enjoyed them. They had organized a choir, which sang several carols. The Chaplain gave the Christmas Story and had prayer.

Then came the big event of the day - Chow! We had another dinner similar to the Thanksgiving one. Ate so much we didn't want to go to chow this evening. Will probably eat a little snack before we go to bed. I will send the Church Bulletin and also the menu. By the way, the menu is part of my work. Ran these off on the ditto machine, enough for each man.

I am still receiving Xmas Cards and as I mentioned before - will try to send them home for you to see. Some of my latest have been from the Willises, Englishes, Walls, Aunt Nonie and Uncle Will, Maurine and Hoffman. Tell all, I really appreciate them. Of course I have received several others too numerous to mention. Guess this about winds up my holiday events so will go on to something else. I did take some pictures today which I will send when I get them developed. We have

the address of some place in Eugene, Oregon where we send our pictures.

Haven't heard anymore from Joe since he left Japan. Suppose he is now in the "Land of the Morning Calm." Do hope he got settled and had a nice day. Think I told you, from what I could gather, he will be located in Teagu, but I could be all wrong.

The weather the past week has been rather pleasant, but it is really turning cold tonight as the wind has begun to blow.

Did I tell you I received a letter from Earl Nagel? He seems to be doing fine and making the best of it. I may have told you this, but can't keep up as the time is going so fast and never can remember the last time I wrote.

Guess I have about covered everything and had better close for this time. Hated to hear about Clovis on his way over and I know it must hurt the Potts. I will be looking forward to hearing of his whereabouts. Hope I can see him as it looks like it will be impossible for Joe and me to get together. Do hope all had a nice Christmas at home and we can look forward to the next one when we all shall be back together once more.

Love to All,
Bill

Wednesday Night

31 December 1952

Dear Mom & All,

Here it is on the eve of a new year. Yes, awaken in the morning and welcome 1953. Really not much to write tonight, but thought a few lines would be welcomed by you. Anyway, it will give me a chance to try out my new ball point pen which is a generous gift I received from the *Paducah Sun Democrat* today.

Received your very nice Christmas box yesterday and appreciate the same. You didn't need to go to all the trouble of wrapping like you did or even send anything for that matter. Would have received it sooner, but the past few days the mail has been all fouled up due to some movements. Also, along with your package yesterday came one from the Fields which contained homemade fudge, gum, fruit cake and orange slices. Was mighty nice of Mrs. and Mr. Fields to do this. Will try to drop them a thank you note soon, but you can pass my thanks on to them. I even received a small box of fudge from Bob Wolff's wife today, so you see we are by all means not hurting for sweets and are probably eating too much.

It started snowing about 4:30 this afternoon and is still at it. I have never seen the ground turn white so quickly as it did this evening. Guess this will be a very good snow. Can't say as I care for it. Snowing on the first of the year will probably mean quite a bit for the rest of the winter.

Suppose you have heard the news about the points being raised to forty. When I first got here, only needed 36, then 38 and now 40. I'm not going to worry until such time I can begin planning on leaving. They could even be lowered by that time.

Still haven't heard from Joe since he was in Japan, but should any day now. Must close for now, but will write more later.

Lots of Love to All,
Bill

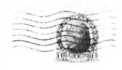

2 January 1953

10:00 p.m.

Dear Mom & All,

This will have to be rather short as I must hit the sack, but will drop a few lines your way first.

In my last letter, I had just received a very nice box from you and it is so nice of you to send it. Well, what happens yesterday, but much to my surprise I received another. This one contained the fruit cake etc. Thanks a million as it all was sure appreciated and wrapped so nicely. Christmas Cards are also still coming my way. Ordinarily all this mail was mailed in time to reach me before Christmas, but due to the rush I am now getting air mail around ten days which isn't so good. Yesterday's mail brought your letter of the 19th so you can see how long it took. Was surprised also by another package yesterday which was a box of fudge from Donna Rea Beavins. I don't think I told you about receiving two pair of wool socks from the Potts or did I?

In today's mail came another Xmas Card from you and enclosed was the pictures. You don't know how glad I was to get them. All are really good. Gene & Marty wrote about their pictures saying they were going to send me one, so I will have a complete set of the family when I get them.

Received a letter from Joe Ned also today telling me about his location and as I thought he is in Taegu. Sure wish I could see him, but the distance is too great. He mentioned seeing a boy I knew from Paducah while he was on the train. Guess he told you about it. He said he mailed the packages when he was home and hoped they beat him here, but evidently they must have traveled with him.

I almost forgot to mention, I received a package from Church today which contained a box of stationery, tooth brush, paste and a new testament. Don't know who was responsible for this but appreciated it also. From what I have written here, you can see I haven't been hurting for mail.

Better sign off as there is no need to start another page.

Lots of Love,
Bill

Monday Night

January 5, 1953

9:15 p.m.

Hello Once Again,

Seems like every time I turn around, it is time to write you once again, but don't know anyone I had rather write to. I received your letter of the 25th today, so when you are so nice to write so often what else can I do, but give out with a few lines. Also received another letter from Joe today, but suppose he is keeping you well posted on his activities.

First of all - I was somewhat shocked at the clipping it contained - meaning Jean Floyd if you have forgotten. I can't claim them all though - Ha! She is a very sweet girl, but was surprised at seeing this. While on the subject of girls, from the Christmas Cards you mentioned receiving, just goes to show how much they all think of my parents and don't forget them. I also received cards from the same. Taking a count of the cards I received now number 36, so you can add this on to yours which should run the number up a ways. I am still receiving them late as it is. Got one today mailed Air Mail on 17 December, so you can see what the Xmas rush did to our mail.

I didn't expect Larry's jacket to get there in time for Xmas, but seems it arrived just right. Am glad it fits as I expected it to be too large as I never did see it. We just saw a sample of a large. Glad he likes it and will try to send something else when I go on R&R, if I ever make it. Could go now if I could find someone to take over my job. Had rather wait until the weather breaks anyway as I don't particularly care about traveling around in this weather.

It made me feel mighty good that the cable ground arrived at such an appropriate time. Was afraid it would be late. We have forms which we can fill out and send back to the APO with the mail clerk. This is how I got the cable ground to you.

Seems that you had a very nice Xmas. Gene and Martha had already told me what they had for the families.

Mom, I can't write anything other than answers to your letters and about mail I receive as there just isn't anything around here to write about.

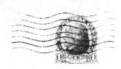

Everyday is the same. Go to bed, get up and work all day. Hardly seems that it should be the 5th already, but as I have said before, the time cannot go too fast to suit me.

Hope all are well and don't work too hard.

Lots of Love,
Bill

CTA082 OB098

O.SFJ271 PD INTL=O.SF TOKYO VIA RCA (48 124)=   DEC 25 PM 1 43

EFM MR MRS W M NACE=

1103 GREER AVE PADUCAH KENTUCKY=

BEST WISHES FOR CHRISTMAS AND NEW YEAR.LOVE TO ALL THE FAMILY.

BILL=

Saturday Night

January 10, 1952

7:30 p.m.

Dear Mom & All,

Received your letter of the 29th today and was very glad to get it as it's the first mail I have received in four days, and even surprised at getting any today as there wasn't much to come in.

Before I sat down to write a few lines, I was just thinking what I could ramble off. As usual, nothing, but will say hello anyway.

I did receive a letter from Earl Nagel the other day and he was supposed to leave the hospital on the 7th or 9th to be returned back to the states. He was thrilled over this, but must be pretty serious to be going back state side. He said they were going to fly him back and he would write me soon as he got settled. Earl's a good kid and I think a lot of him, sure hope everything comes out all right for him.

This won't sound quite right for Korea, but the temperature reached a big 40 degrees here today. After being so cold, this was just like spring. Don't imagine it will last too long. Things sure turned muddy in a hurry as all has been frozen for such a long period. Didn't realize there was so much moisture in the ground.

Like I said, nothing to write about so there isn't any need of rambling on. Hardly seems possible today should be the 10th, but glad to see them fly by. I certainly did enjoy reading about your nice Xmas and glad everything worked out so well.

I will try to write more in a few days. Hope all are well and not working too hard. Tell everyone hello for me.

Lots of Love,
Bill

PS. The picture is an extra one that one of the guys had and gave to me. This is all we see, one hill after another.

Wednesday

January 14, 1953

Dear Mom & All,

Should have answered your letter last night which I received yesterday, but as usual nothing to write about, so thought I would wait until today – still nothing worth while, but here goes anyway.

Mom, don't feel bad about my not receiving your packages until after Xmas as I understand it wasn't your fault and I thought nothing about it. I still have food left as I received so much and was glad it did come later. They were mailed at the same time and got here a couple of days apart, so that shows what the mail situation was around that time. If I'm not mistaken, there was another letter in between the ones you spoke of. Hope it finally reached you. I received one Xmas card which was mailed on 10th of Dec - Air Mail - and I didn't get it until 4th of Jan.

Was glad to hear you had such a wonderful time at the Throgmortons and being with the Poores.

It has really been cold here the past few days and down to zero most of the time. Think in my last letter I said the temperature was 40 degrees which we all were enjoying, but didn't last long.

I had a letter from Ernest Walls today which I enjoyed very much. He certainly does write nice letters. He told me all about their Xmas and what was going on at the bank. Haven't heard from Joe Ned in about a week. His last letter, he still hadn't gone to work and was waiting on some kind of an assignment.

Glad I waited until today to write as I received some pictures which I sent back to the states to be developed. Won't send them all at once, but a few at a time. Maybe you can enjoy them more this way. At least it will give me something to send when there is nothing to write.

Guess this will be all for this time as this is about the latest with me. Sure hope the strike doesn't come off and everything is straightened out once more.

Love to All,

Bill

Sunday Night

January, 18, 1953

Hello "Old Chap"

How's the baby brother doing? Received your letter of the 5th today along with Mom's and certainly was good to hear from both of you. Will dash off a few lines to you tonight and will try to write Mom tomorrow.

Really glad you liked the jacket. Of course I never did see it, only the sample. Keep it nice until I get home. Would like to have one like it for myself. When I go on R&R to Japan, I will try to send you something else I can pick out. Doesn't look as if I will get to go before Spring. It will be a better time of the year to go anyway.

Your picture Mom sent is really good and I'm mighty proud of it to have such a good and nice looking brother as you. Just kidding about the Baby Brother above, because you have really grown as I can tell from the picture. How many girls got one like it!

I don't know too much about the motor scooter. My advice to you is to forget about this and use all that money in some other way. While you are making good money I would hold onto it. Won't be too long before you will be old enough to drive. Will let you have my car then. I saw a picture of the new "Chev" today and it looks pretty nice.

Larry, try to drop a few lines more often and let me in on what you are doing, such as your grades, girl friends, etc. Don't tell me you don't have any. Has your work been interfering with your grades?

Be good and I will try to write more later. Here's a couple of pictures one of me and my buddy on the outpost.

As Ever,

Bill

Monday Night

January 19, 1953

Dear Mom & All,

Received your letter dated the 7th yesterday but answered Larry's last night so decided to wait until this time to answer yours. There isn't much to write about as usual, but will give a few lines anyway. The mail situation is still fouled up and takes me about ten days to receive a letter at the present time. Would like to know how long it is taking mine to reach you.

I had a very nice letter from Omar Willis yesterday and he is over in this sector once more, so maybe we will see each other yet. Sure hope so! He wanted to know all about what Joe Ned was doing and where he is located. He mentioned receiving your Xmas Card and told me to thank you the next time I wrote. He certainly did appreciate it. Also received a letter from the Barbers yesterday. They told me how much they enjoyed eating with you and what a good meal you had.

You mentioned Aunt Blanche still working, I didn't even know she had gone to work. Maybe there is a letter I haven't received from you, or then again suppose you could be like me - can't remember who you wrote to about what. I find this very true in my case. What kind of work is she doing?

Went to church services yesterday and as usual enjoyed them very much. We had a visiting Chaplain from another outfit as ours was out somewhere. His service was very nice, but I think our Chaplain is a better speaker even though he is colored.

As I said to begin with, this wouldn't be much, but will just let you know I'm doing fine and can't complain. I trust all is well with all at home and tell everyone hello. Will enclose a couple more pictures just to add something to this short letter.

Lots of Love,
Bill

Monday Night

January 10, 1953

Dear Mom & All,

Guess you are somewhat surprised to hear from me again so soon as it was only last night I wrote, but today I received your letter of the 11th and will waste no time in answering it.

I was somewhat surprised at your letter as there is no need to worry about me. You know this is the last thing I want any of you to do as I am all right and making out fine. I want you to consider me just away from home at work for this is no more than just a job to me. Like you, I keep faith in the Lord and with His guidance I find things much easier. You know what my plans are when I return home, so my time served here I feel may be of benefit to me later on.

Maybe you noticed the outside of the envelope which I addressed last evening. First I thought I would see how long it took you to notice it, but after getting your letter today and your worrying about not getting one of my letters, you might think you didn't receive one telling of my promotion. Yes, I finally made Cpl. Of course the rank doesn't mean a whole lot to me, but I can always use a little extra money.

Also in the mail today came a letter from Clovis. He is still at Ft. Lawton and is being held there for some medical check ups. Didn't say what was wrong with him, but he expected to ship out around the 15th. I have never received a letter that pleased me more than this one. From the way he wrote, that boy now has a different outlook on life. Of course I always considered him as my best friend. He really wrote a wonderful letter.

I had better close for now as I think I have done well writing two pages. Will throw in a couple more pictures.

Love to All,

Bill

Saturday Night

January 24, 1953

Dear Mom & All,

Just a few lines once again. Still nothing new with me, but beings as I have a few minutes will say hello and goodbye at the least.

I received a nice long letter from Marty and Gene yesterday and enclosed was the very good picture of them. My pictures of the family are now complete and I thank all of you. I really have a swell, good looking family even in pictures and they help out very much. Also in Gene and Marty's letters were the clippings of the big fire. From the pictures I can imagine what a mass of ruins were left.

About the best news I have at the present time - if things don't change, I am scheduled for R&R the 3rd of February. I will go to Tokyo having five big days there and I plan on doing nothing but eat and sleep. Of course I'm just kidding about that as I plan on sight seeing also. Two of my very good friends - one in A Btry. and the other in B Btry. are also scheduled for Tokyo at this time. I was very glad to hear of this as they both are two swell, very good guys and the three of us should have an excellent time, provided the weather is nice

I had a nice letter from Mrs. Potts yesterday and they are all doing well outside of worrying about Clovis. Suppose it is in parents to do so, although we don't want you to do it. I still want you and Dad to drive down there some Sunday. Take the Taylors along with you.

Don't think I mentioned to you, we all had an influenza shot the other day. So far I have been fortunate and escaped all sickness outside of minor colds and hope to continue to do so.

I didn't intend to start another page and don't expect to get much on it.

By the way, I might tell you what purpose the can which the fruit cake was in is now serving. We have been popping corn in it. One of the fellows received corn, popping oil and salt from home, so last night the problem of how to pop it was solved. The can worked perfect and we enjoyed the corn.

I must close for now as I don't know how I wrote this much. Forgot to mention I received a letter from Dewey Young yesterday which I certainly appreciated. Also Mrs. Fields added a few lines to Gene and Marty's letters as she was there at that time. Appreciated her doing so. I really think a lot of her as she has always been so swell to me.

Lots of Love,
Bill

Thursday Night

January 29, 1953

Dear Mon & All,

Received your letter of the 18th a couple of days ago, but this is the first chance I have had to answer it as I was rather busy at that time. The pictures I appreciated very much and just finished a short letter to Joe Ned forwarding them to him. I thought they were very good and always enjoy receiving pictures. Does Kenneth have his camera with him? If not would like for you to make a few pictures.

The reason I didn't answer sooner was because we have been in the mess of moving. I just happened to think, I haven't even answered your letter of the 13th which I received on the 26th. We didn't move too far, but even at that it is still a big mess just like moving at home. We moved at night and of course didn't get any sleep, but I got a full nights sleep last night and feel fine now. The new area is about the same as the other as I have said before, all Korea is just alike in this area. We do have some trees over here where the hills in the other area were all bare. It started snowing soon after we reached the position which made things much worse, but we are pretty well straightened out now. Next Tuesday I am still looking towards R&R and figure this will be a good time to go as the Battery should he pretty well set up once more when I return.

I didn't know that Joe Ned had sent Larry a jacket, but so glad they are different. He should be quite the sport - Ha!

You figured about right on my points. At the end of this month I will have 22 which is over half way provided they don't raise them again. If they raise them anymore I will get out on ETS. Just add three points to this total each month if you want to know how many I do have.

This has been very short and not much news, but thought I had better write a few lines anyway. Don't worry about my welfare, because if I'm ever sick I will let you know. I have been fortunate thus far and hope to continue this way. Must close for now and shave.

Lots of Love,
Bill

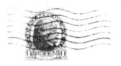

Thursday Night

February, 5, 1953

Dear Mom,

Here I have received two letters from you once again before I have gotten around to writing. I haven't written a letter now in about a week, because I really haven't had the time strange as it might seem and then again as usual nothing to write about. We got behind in our work during the move and I have been trying to catch up.

To top things off, you can see by the date of this letter I didn't make R&R as planned. I was pulled off because we had a change in Sergeants and I was the only one who knew what was going on. They said they couldn't hold me back, but didn't know how they would operate without me, so for the benefit of the organization I had to put it off once more. It really didn't make a lot of difference with me as it has been too cold for moving around, so now I guess I will wait until Spring for R&R. This makes me sound rather important, but that's the way it is - Ha!

We are about to get straightened out once more after our move. Think I told you I am now living in a bunker. We had one already built over here and it is rather nice. It sure beats living in a tent as they are so much warmer.

About my mustache, I didn't even think about it being in the pictures as I have had it since November. Just something different and I will shave it off before coming home, so don't think anything about this. Practically everyone has acquired such.

I don't know any reason for the mail situation being like it is, but yesterday I received your letter of the 27th and today came the one written on the 22nd, so that's the way it goes. The one I received yesterday had Cpl. on it and the one today Pfc. I can see my little brother is very observing seeing Cpl. on the envelope.

I just stepped outside and it is beginning to snow. Sure hope it isn't much.

Looks as if I never will see Omar Willis. After him getting in my vicinity once more, we move out, so that's the way it happens every time.

I now have a new detail to take care of each day. I am in charge of putting up and taking the flag down with the help of two others. We put

it up at seven in the morning and take it down at five in the evening.

I must close for now and I promise to do a little better on my letter writing, but don't ever worry if you go for a while without hearing from me. Hope all are well and doing fine.

Lots of Love,
Bill

Tuesday Night

February 10, 1953

10:00 p.m.

Dear Mom & All,

Suppose you are wondering once again what has happened to those so called wonderful letters of mine you speak of. I'm sorry I haven't written sooner, but the reason why is that I just haven't had the time to write anyone in the last week or so. I have been working every night since we moved and seems the more I work the more there is to do. I am now tied up with the papers on another court martial which was tried Saturday night plus everything else. Of course we have a deadline on such things and they have to be taken care of. No one seems to know how to do such things and I have to take care of them. Sometimes I wish I didn't know them. Maybe before too long we will get caught up once again and I will have a little more time to write.

I received your most welcomed letter of the 1st today along with pictures. I appreciate the pictures as well as the letter and will forward the pictures on to Joe. I also had a letter from him today and one from the Potts.

Mrs. Potts said Clovis was to ship out on the 3rd of this month, so I suppose he is well on the way by now. They were really feeling blue about this as I could tell from the letter. Sure hope Clovis gets located somewhere I can see him.

What a surprise it was to receive the clipping you enclosed. I was very much shocked by this as she had told me she wasn't going to get married. If I don't get home soon there isn't going to be any girls left for me. Ha!

The weather continues to be about the same here. Tonight it has been trying to snow once again.

I wish I had more to write about, but I'm rather tired and must close for now. Will try to write more soon. I am doing well and feeling fine. Hope all at home are the same.

Lots of Love,
Bill

Friday Night

Feb 13, 1953

6:30

Dear Mom & All,

Once again I will try dropping a few lines your way. As usual, nothing worth while to write about, but suppose I had better write while having the time.

The weather has really been nice for the past few days -just like Spring. Sure wish it would stay this way, but know it is hopeless this time of the year. I want summer to roll around as I will know then it will not be too long until I should be leaving. Tomorrow, this month will be half gone and that hardly seems possible.

Before too long, I should have a little more time for writing. The reason being in about two weeks I plan on changing jobs. I will really be glad to give this one up, although I know it very well, but that is just the trouble. It's by request of the Battery Commander that I will be changing. The officer I am now working under doesn't want to let me go, but the Battery Commander wants me to come down and run his supply for him. I don't know the first thing about it, but he says I won't have any trouble learning and I feel I can better myself by doing so. I already have a new man which I'm breaking in on this job, so I guess it is official. By taking this position there is a slim chance I could make sergeant before coming home.

I had a very nice long letter from Mrs. Potts yesterday or suppose it was the day before. I may have already told you, she said Clovis was to leave the States the 3rd.

By changing jobs, I should be able to give R&R a try before too long again. At least I don't think they could declare me essential. Will also have a little more money to spend after getting paid this month.

Guess I had better bring this to a close so I might have a little more to write about next time. Hope all are well and tell everyone hello.

Lots of Love,
Bill

P.S. I forgot to mention about the pictures you sent - That cake sure looked good. I even noticed each little article, such as ash trays - Ha!

Sunday Night

February 15, 1953

7:30 p.m.

Dear Mom & All,

Yesterday I received your very pretty Valentine and thought it really a coincidence to receive it on Valentines Day the way the mail has been coming. Thanks very much for thinking of me.

Then today the cookies came, which were only a day late. They are really good as we are putting them away at the present time. The three guys in the bunker send their thanks also and said they are very good.

This morning I went to Chapel Services and enjoyed them very much. I was just thinking, back in the summer I wrote and told about sitting out in the hot sun attending services and now its in a cold squad tent, but we are still enjoying the services.

As I think I told you in my last letter, we have had pretty weather for the past week or so, but this morning it was very cold once again. Shouldn't be too long now until we will be having a few nice days along with the bad ones.

Yesterday, the section with which I work moved into the new bunker which has just been completed. It is very nice except for the fact we are pretty crowded. Almost like a state side office now although built from scraps of whatever we could find around over the place. I kind of hate to leave the section now that they have a pretty good set up, but had still rather go to supply work. Have a better chance for advancement there or at least have the chance, where as I have gotten all I can on the present job.

As usual, this hasn't been much of a letter, but wanted to thank you for the Valentine and cookies. Will try to write more often, though my letters will be shorter.

Lots of Love,
Bill

P.S. I forgot to mention, I received ten newspapers today, so have been reading up on the latest news. I do enjoy looking through them, late as they come.

Friday Night

February 20, 1953

10:00 p.m.

Dear Mom & All,

Received your letter of the 10th today and welcomed it as usual. I had planned on writing tonight anyway, so that made things even better when your letter arrived.

I started to work on my new job yesterday and think I will like it fine. I don't feel like I'm as pressed or pinned down here and have a little more space time. Another thing, it gives me a chance to get out a little as I will have to make runs to different places picking up supplies. There is quite a bit to learn, but don't think it will take me long.

Another big thing, if all works out this time, I will be going on R&R the 25th. Once again it will be Tokyo. By the time you receive this letter I should be having a great time there. I haven't planned too much on it until the 25th comes, as I saw what happened last time.

Was surprised at my promotion being announced over the radio. We had to fill out all this information on a form, but had no idea it would go that far. Guess this Army has a pretty good set up in some ways.

Enjoyed the clippings about the weddings, but then again hate to see all these good looking girls getting married. Ha! The guy Bobbye Stivers married must have got a special leave from Germany just to come back to the states to get married. What a racket the Air Force has.

I haven't heard from Joe Ned in quite some while, but suppose he is doing fine and like myself there is nothing to write about.

Had better close for this time and write again before I depart on R&R. Will try to write some while in Japan, but if you don't hear from me during that time you will know the reason.

Tell all hello - Lots of Love,
Bill

Saturday Night

March 7, 1953

7.30 p.m.

Dear Mom & All,

Sorry this won't be as long as my last one, but I'm about written out answering all the mail I had waiting for me upon my return. I wanted to send some more pictures anyway, so thought I could drop a few lines in answer to your letter of the 25th which I received yesterday. Really enjoyed it, being so nice and long, but no matter how much you write, your letters are always so pleasing.

I was very much surprised at all the big changes of the Midwest Office, but then everyone must have been from what you wrote. However, I wasn't a bit surprised at them choosing you to keep, because they knew you took an interest in your job. You remember my telling Dad when you first went to work, they wouldn't find anyone that had the interest of the Co., and would do their best like you would. I can imagine there will be a lot of work to do now, but by all means, don't work too hard and let it get the best of you. I am so happy you enjoy your work the way you do and doing so well with it, but then like you say, it isn't a necessity of you working and if ever too much, don't hesitate about quitting.

Today has been rainy and windy. This so far has really been a typical March. The weather here reminds me a whole lot of Kentucky. Maybe just my imagination, but find it quite true.

Will sign off for now and begin thinking about hitting the sack as I was on guard last night and didn't get much sleep. I don't have to walk a post now as I pull Cpl. of the guard, but have to be up just the same.

Tell all hello and will try to make my next letter a little more interesting.

Lots of Love,
Bill

On R&R in Tokyo, Japan

Thursday Night

March 15, 1953

6:45 p.m.

Dear Mom & All,

Here I am back in Korea after five wonderful days in Japan. I really had a nice time outside of the trip over and coming back which was rather rough. I am sorry it has been so long since I wrote, but I didn't write anyone while I was on R&R. Even wanted to get away from this for a while.

Now to tell you a little about my trip as it would take all night to tell it all. First we left here around 5:30 p.m. on the 25th and went about 25 miles by truck to Sintan-ni Railhead. We left the Railhead around 11:00 p.m. and arrived in Seoul by train around 5:00 a.m. on the 26th. From here we were carried to Seoul Airport. We stayed around there until 4:00 p.m. and at which time we boarded a plane headed for Tokyo. It took us exactly four hours to fly from Seoul to Tokyo. Pretty good time as there were about two hundred aboard the plane.

From Tokyo Airport we were put on buses and carried to Camp Drake. We entered the building there and marched straight to the dinning room where we were fed a big steak with all the trimmings plus milk and ice cream. I don't know as I ever enjoyed a meal anymore than this one though it was on an Army tray. Of course the time I eat yours again will beat this.

After this we began processing. Took a good hot shower and given a complete change of clothes and a uniform. I never knew Army ODs could feel so wonderful and comfortable - Ha! It was close to 11:00 p.m. when we finished processing and from Drake we were carried to the R&R Center in Yokohama by bus.

This was really a nice place and we could stay there all five days for $1.75 with meals and all. The huts held about twenty guys and were named for the different states. Here we had everything, barber shop, PX, snack bar, picture developing, shoe shine, mess hall with Japanese girls as waitresses and boys to make our beds. The only thing it was still under Army operation, nice as it was, so myself and a friend stayed there a couple of nights and then went to Tokyo and rented a hotel room

which was real nice, just to have a room of your own for a change.

The first day was spent grooming. By this I mean hair-cut, shampoo, shave, face massage and even a manicure. Went all out. I was too lazy to shave myself the whole time while there, so each day I got a shave for 15 cents. Although 15 cents you could never get a shave like that in Paducah. Haircuts were only 25 cents, so I got one the first day I was there and one the last day. Talking about this good shave, I can say for the Japanese people whatever their trade is, they take great pains in it and are very skilled even to driving a car.

While there I did quite a bit of shopping and went to a movie a couple of nights. Of course there is no need in saying I did some big eating also. Steaks, Chicken, anything I wanted and very cheap at that, which was at the Rocker-Four Club in Tokyo strictly for GIs. You will receive a picture made while there.

Four of us guys took a tour in a '48 Ford the second day there and saw all the interesting places which I took pictures of and will send to you a few at a time. This was very nice as we really traveled around Tokyo for only a thousand yen a piece which is about $3.60 in our money. Well worth it.

As you know, the Japanese drive on the left hand side of the street. I don't see how they keep from having more accidents than they do. They couldn't drive without a horn as they bare down on it and keep going. Quite some noise.

I sent a box of goods home addressed to myself, but for you to open and put away. This includes a jacket, robe, smoking jacket, photo album for all my pictures. Knowing that Gene had already sent you all the glorious garb of Japan there wasn't anything I knew of to send you, but mailed a table cloth anyway. In the same package is a billfold for Dad and Larry as I didn't know what else to send them. Think maybe they can use them as I bought myself one. I sent Kenneth a lounging jacket which I think will go over with a college student. Just like the one I got myself. Don't think Martha has a Komona, so I sent her this plus a pair of pajamas and Gene a nice bathrobe. Jimmy told me while in Gary if I ever got the chance to send Virginia a Komona, so not forgetting this I did so, and sent Jimmy a lounging jacket. Not leaving, Aunt Blanche and Uncle James out, just a small remembrance of a table cloth to them and one each for Ruth Ann and Carol Lee. May seem to you I did a lot of buying, but things were all so pretty, different and

even at that cheap and all have been so nice to me I felt like doing this. Sounds funny but I rather like spending money again and I had saved for this a little at a time since being here.

I ran into a couple of guys in Japan I went through basic and leadership with and two more on the way back at Seoul Airport. From them I found out about all the guys as most everyone stuck together except me and I consider myself fortunate.

After all the wonderful time, we left the R&R Center around 7:30 p.m. March 3, and had to report back to Drake at midnight. We had to wait around there to start processing until about 2:00 a.m. Hated to pull off the ODs and get back into fatigues, but that's the way it had to be. After this it was about 4:00 a.m. and we were fed a big breakfast of ham and eggs, toast, cereal etc. From here we were carried to Tokyo Air Port once again, put on the plane, but this time headed back for Korea. We landed at Seoul about 9:30 a.m. and had to wait around there until 6:30 p.m. to get the train back to the Railhead. This is a long slow ride and we got to Sintan-ni about 3:00 a.m. this morning where we were met by our trucks and brought back to the outfit, so you can see what I mean about the trip. Think I have done a pretty fair job of covering everything and hope it hasn't been too boring. Not often I get to write a long letter and expect this will be the last lengthy one for sometime. It will take me a month to get caught up on my correspondence as I had fifteen letters waiting when I returned, two of which were yours,

I was so glad you had such an enjoyable time at Bloomington. Will hear all about it again from Gene & Marty. I know their apartment is nice and I'm looking forward to seeing it.

You mentioned the weather being so nice while at Bloomington, it was just like Spring the first couple of days in Japan, but cloudy and misting rain the other three. Really wanted to take more pictures, but too cloudy. I meant to tell you, I weighed while there and almost fell over when I saw the scales -you would never guess - 175 lbs. This means fifteen lbs. while in Korea and 40 lbs. since being in the Army. I had better stop before I get fat - Ha!

Since you want to know, my food supply is just about exhausted and I could always use more but don't like for you to go to the trouble. I tell you what I have wished for so many times and wonder if it would be possible to send. Think nothing of it if too much trouble, but one of

those black walnut cherry cakes would taste good. Anytime you want to send anything go right ahead

One of the letters I had was from Clovis, but written while he was on ship. I am anxious to know where he is located.

What a letter! Had better close and answer a few others, such as Gene & Marty, Garland, Dewey Young, Kenneth, Nancy Reaves (a girl in Dyersburg) are among letters I had waiting. Hope all are well and the packages should arrive in about a month.

Lots of Love,
Bill

Dear Mom & All,

Think this is the first time I have ever written a letter during the morning hours. The reason being, I now have a new job in addition to my other. This consists of selling items out of the PX as we call it. Of course all it is, is cigarettes, candy, can goods or such items as we get in our rations. Not a whole lot to it, but sell these items between the hours of 6:30-9:30 and have to keep up with all the money and merchandise. I told them I would take it provided nothing was said about me writing letters in the day time, when there was nothing else to do, so this explains my writing at this time. Another thing, I won't have to pull any guard doing this job.

I received your nice long letter along with the pictures which were taken in Bloomington. As you say, I will exchange the pictures with Joe Ned. I thought them to be very good and appreciate your sending them. If that Larry doesn't quit growing, he is going to be taller than you by the time I get home. I also noticed his hair cut. Think it look's very good on him.

From what you write about the office, reminds me a whole lot of this Army. Always changing things around, moving this and moving that, and you went on to say, you never knew one day where you would be the next, and that's just the way it is here. As I keep telling you just keep with it, until such time as it comes to be too much and then quit. You are really doing well, and I'm always glad to hear about your work and to know you are so interested in it.

Glad you had such a nice time in Mayfield and hope Aunt Lulye's and Mary Lou's plans worked out and they got to visit with you. If so, I know all had a swell time and enjoyed themselves.

Everything is going as usual with me. Another month will soon be over, which means three more points to my credit. They are really building up. Just think, in six more days, or by the time you receive this, I will have been gone from home ten months. This hardly seems possible. It is rumored that the points will drop to 38 again in the near future, but I'm not planning on it, because as I say, it is only a rumor.

Guess the Spring rains will be coming before too long. It rained most of the day yesterday and about half the night. Is cloudy again today.

Had better sign off for this time, as this about covers the news if that's what you want to call it. I still have a few pictures left so will enclose them with this letter.

Lots of Love,
Bill

Saturday Morn

March 28, 1953

9:30 a.m.

Dear Mom & All,

Received your very nice letter of the 17th a couple of days ago and sorry I haven't answered sooner. Once again I find myself so busy, can't find much time to write. I owe a letter to Gene and Marty, Kenneth, Jimmy and Virginia. Also, the first of the week I received a nice box of Easter Candy from Mrs. Fields. It really is nice of her to think of me in this way and I sure appreciate it. I must write her a letter thanking her.

Joe Ned has probably already written you, but if all works out, he plans to make the trip up and visit with me around the 2nd of April. All the paper work on this has been taken care of as his CO sent a letter to my CO, asking for permission to let him visit the area. Of course there was no trouble at this end. He seems to have all his transportation lined up, so I hope all works out.

Even if he can only stay one day, I am really looking forward to seeing him. We will let you know what happens. If its pretty we will make some pictures together.

I knew Bobby Gates had gone home. So glad you got to hear him on the radio. He, as you say, is really a nice boy.

I was very much surprised to hear about Mama & Papa Nace being grandparents again and even more surprised when you said it was Eulaine. I know everyone is thrilled over this event.

This has been mighty short, but just wanted to dash off a few lines to let you know I'm doing fine. Please excuse this and I will try to do better next time.

Lots of Love,
Bill

P.S. Hope all have a nice Easter!

April 4, 1953

Dear Mom & Pop,

Tonight finds me spending my second night in the 9th FA Bn., which I know all of you will welcome as good news. Yesterday my little leave started, and was I surprised when they gave me 7 days. My trip up was easy and I enjoyed every bit of it. I caught a plane at Taegu about 11:00 o'clock and an hour and a half later I was in Seoul. I waited there until 4:15 and then got a light plane that brought me to the 3rd Div. Air Strip. From there I called Bill and he hustled over and picked me up. You can bet his voice sounded good over the phone and then it was even better when he came up to meet me. Honestly, he looks better than he ever has. You can believe his reports about gaining weight for he has certainly filled out, and he is getting broad as a beam across the shoulders.

Last night we just sat around and talked and did the same most of today. Bill hasn't worked much today, and has taken me on a tour of the area. We took a few pictures which I suppose you shall see shortly. Their life here is nothing as "lavish" (I use the word loosely) as ours, but I am surprised at the set-up they do have here. Their living facilities are much better than I expected to find.

Right now Bill is working in the PX, but I think, he plans to send a few lines along with this.

Tomorrow is Easter and I am very grateful that on this special day Bill and I were able to be together so far from home. We plan to go to sunrise services in the morning, and I'm sure it will be an occasion we shall never forget. I thank the Lord that it is possible.

Tuesday I was very surprised to receive another package from you and even more surprised to find a cake inside. It was certainly an ingenious manner in which you sent it, and it arrived in good condition and wonderful - nothing in a long time has been quite so good, What was even better, Bill still had part of his last night and I had another piece. I express my thanks for both of us.

Both you and Pop seem to be doing rather well in the line of recent monetary gains. What do you plan to do with all the extra cash. Really I'm proud for you both and I know you deserve all that you get.

I'll stop for now and let Bill take over for a few lines. I'll not have to leave before Wednesday, so I'll write again before I leave.

Love to All,
Joe Ned

Saturday Night

April 4, 1953

8:30 p.m.

Dear Mom & All,

Looks as if Joe has about covered all the latest events, but will add my few lines anyway. You can't imagine how thrilled I was when he called. It has really done me good to see and be with him.

I can also say that he is looking good and hasn't changed one bit. I, too, was surprised at him getting such a long leave, but we can sure put it to good use. Of course there isn't a whole lot to offer up here, but we are together and that's the main thing.

Yes, like Joe said in his letter I feel that it was a work of the Lord that two brothers could spend Easter Sunday together over here. Sure hope tomorrow is pretty as we are going to attend Sunrise Services. This day we shall always cherish and remember, the Easter of 1953.

I had to laugh tonight as Joe was standing in the PX and one of the fellows in there said to his buddy, that I and the guy over there could pass for twins. He was quite surprised when I told him we were brothers.

I had been holding off on answering your last letter as I was expecting Joe and thought this would add a little news. In fact I was expecting him on the second and even went as far as to set up a cot for him. I was somewhat disappointed when he didn't show up as I thought perhaps he didn't make it.

We are really having a swell time together talking over old times and this and that. We took several pictures today and will take more before he leaves. These pictures, I'm sure both of us will want to keep always.

You can bet we are proud of our Mom and Dad doing so well in their work. Both raises are a pretty big jump, but I'm sure well earned.

I realize my letter hasn't been as long as Joe's, but he covered about everything and afraid mine is more or less just a repetition, but will say once more, I am thankful to the Lord for making Joe's visit possible and especially at this time of the year.

I want to thank you for the nice Easter Cards and your cakes are still as good as ever if not better. I am not stretching the issue. One of the fellows said it was the best he had ever eaten. I hope this finds all of you doing well and hope you found your Easter Season as enjoyable as ours.

Lots of Love,
Bill

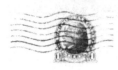

Tuesday Night

April 7, 1953

9:00 p.m.

Dear Mom & All,

Just a few lines tonight to let you know Joe & I have really had a swell time together. This is his last night here, so thought we had better send another letter your way.

I received your very nice letter yesterday or should say two letters as one was written on the bank statement. I appreciated your sending the statement and also the clippings and of course I didn't have to send them on to Joe as he was right here to read them. Yes, it was quite a coincidence that my letter asking about George and Don arrived the day he was there. Glad you all had such a nice time and I know George enjoyed being with you.

Other mail which I have received since last writing, included Easter Cards from Mrs. Dunbar and Mr. & Mrs. Robert Pierce. Really was nice of them to think of me and I appreciated this very much.

Joe & I attended Sunrise Services and also regular Service Easter. Both were really inspiring and I was so thankful we could worship together on Easter even in Korea. We will enclose the bulletin with this letter.

My work has had to go on just the same although Joe has been here, but I sure have enjoyed his visit. Wish there was more I could have done to show him a good time, but think he has found all interesting and seeing what I am doing. We have taken several pictures which you will receive later on.

Guess this is about the best I can do for now, so will let Joe take over and add a little more. Hope all is settled down once more at the Mid-West establishment and things are back to normal.

Lots of Love,
Bill

Seems that Bill has just about covered everything that has happened in the past few days, so I'll not add much more than my hello.

I certainly have enjoyed my visit with him here. Of course the main thing was just seeing him, but in the bargain I have seen more of Korea and have learned a few of the interesting activities of an artillery battery. Another thing is that it has given me a few days respite from my day to day routine. I honestly hate to return and start to work once more.

But now the time is growing slimmer day by day and I can say that next month I shall be starting for home. Then when I leave Bill will have about as much time to go as I presently have.

We both want you to know that this has been one of the most wonderful experiences in our lives, and one we can always look back on and be thankful for. I'm sorry it must end, but very soon now we can all be back together once more.

Goodnight for now and our love to all.
Joe Ned

Wednesday Night

April 15, 1953

9:30 p.m.

Dear Mom & All,

Suppose it is about time I dropped a line or two your way. I didn't realize it had been so long until I got to thinking the last letter was written while Joe was still here which has been over a week ago.

I certainly did hate to see Joe leave as we were together for almost a week and I really missed him for awhile. I carried him back to the Air Strip and haven't heard from him since his return. Sure hope he had as much luck going back as he did coming up. There really isn't any need of writing our COs, but they knew how happy we were to get together.

I am glad all of you had such a nice Easter, because as I said before, mine couldn't have been any better. Joe and I shall never forget spending Easter together in Korea. Of course there wasn't any need of your sending thanks for your Orchid. Only wish I could have seen you. I do feel rather badly about one thing after writing Dad about the flowers, I forgot to mention his birthday. However, I didn't forget about it as Joe and I both spoke of it, but just neglected to mention it. Late as it is, will say Happy Birthday! Guess he has quit having birthdays anyway. Ha.

I have been wondering why Albert Jones never did write anymore. It certainly was nice of him to come by and visit with you. If he is having a hard time getting adjusted to school life again I imagine I will have a time after being out so long.

Well, I was very surprised when Paducah made the headlines in *Stars & Strips* newspaper today. This was about the 3,000,000 blast at Joppa Steam Plant. Those people around there had better be careful or I will be afraid to come home.

I hate to sit down and write a letter now as there is nothing worth while to say. Your letters are always so long and interesting. I do well if I write to anyone else now on this account. Just can't seem to get in the writing mood.

I don't think I mentioned it and don't know whether Joe did, but I talked him out of his watch when he was here. Oh, I didn't talk him out of it, but I was badly in need of one since mine has been broken since

Oct. This is the watch Dad bought for him before he went into the Army. Joe said he was going to get another one, a nice dress watch, which he could get at the PX in Taegu. I offered to pay him for this one, but he wouldn't take it. At least it is still in the family and hope Dad doesn't mind him giving the watch away. Ha!

Looks like I have done fairly well on one of these short letters for a change. Don't think I have said much, but anyway I have filled three pages.

I will be looking forward to the can goods and will let you know when I receive them. Thanks for going to the trouble. Enough for tonight.

Lots of Love,
Bill

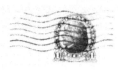

Friday Night

April 24, 1953

8:00 p.m.

Dear Mom & All,

Received your most wonderful long letter of the 13th a couple of days ago. I don't know when I have enjoyed a letter so much. Of course I enjoy all your letters, but in this one, you had received the news about Joe and me and then told of your visit with the Potts.

I am so glad you finally broke loose and got to go to Dyersburg. Now you know why I always like to go. I know the Potts were more than happy to have you as they think so much of you and have said so often they wanted you and Dad to visit with them.

Today I received all the pictures from Joe which were taken during our visit. Most of them turned out real well and will forward them on to you.

This has really been a Spring Day. Hope the weather continues like it has been. The days are getting so much longer now also.

I hate to put this in an envelope after getting your six page letter, but wanted to send the pictures as I know you are anxious to see them.

Will sign off for now and I will try to write more real soon.

Lots of Love,
Bill

Saturday Night

April 25, 1953

6:30 p.m.

Dear Mom & All,

No news other than what I wrote last night, but just wanted to send a few more pictures and will say hello while doing so.

Today has been another beautiful, but windy Spring day. This is the time of year I always like. Of course the best time of this year will be when I get home.

Won't be long before I, too, can be counting the days. I really don't care about doing this as that makes the time go slow sure enough.

Well, I said I was only going to say hello, so will let it go at that.

Lots of Love,
Bill

P.S. The pictures with snow were already on my roll of film when Joe got here.

Sunday Night

April 26, 1953

9:00 p.m.

Dear Mom & All,

Don't be surprised at another letter so soon, but I want to get the pictures home and might as well add a few lines along with them.

I received your letter of the 17th today, so you can consider this as an answer to it, short as it might be. You said it didn't contain any news, but your letters are always welcomed and so interesting.

This morning I attended out door services and might add we had communion. Really a nice service and such a beautiful day. So many of the hills are covered with pretty pink bushes which resemble the red bud trees. I am really glad to see things showing signs of Spring. Even makes one feel so much better.

I will agree with you that the nearer time comes for me to rotate the slower it seems to go, but we can't wish for that time to get here, because as the saying goes, we are only wishing our lives away. With the points staying at 40, it will be sometime near the end of July before I leave, however, between now and then I am hoping they will drop back to 38 and I will get out of here the 1st of July.

I can't imagine you having snow flurries at the time your letter was written as sometime ago you mentioned having 86 degree temperature. Sure hope all of our cold weather is over.

Had better quit for this time and enclose a few pictures. Eventually, I will get them all home.

Lots of Love,
Bill

Monday Night

April 27, 1953

10:00 p.m.

Dear Mom & All,

Yes, just me again with a few more pictures. Perhaps you are hoping the pictures won't run out as it is one way for me to drop a few lines.

Another beautiful day describes this one and plenty warm. I even took the sand bags from around the bottom of the tent today and rolled up the sides, so Spring must really be here. The roads are once again full of dust and beginning to remind me of last Summer. Guess I will eat quite a bit more of it before I get out of here. Nevertheless, I will still prefer the Summer to the Winters over here.

I really received a nice long letter front Albert Jones today. He told me about his visit with you and how much he enjoyed it.

The pictures I am sending in this letter, Joe must have taken on his way up here. I never knew there was such a nice place in Korea as the hut in one of the pictures. I am glad he took the pictures of the plane as this is the kind I flew to Tokyo on and I didn't have a chance to snap any. Quite a plane and can carry quite a few passengers as well as cargo. Notice how the nose opens up to form the entrance.

This is it for tonight as time is growing late and I must shave before retiring. Will try to send some more tomorrow.

Lots of Love,
Bill

Tuesday Night

April 28, 1953

9:45 p.m.

Dear Mom & All,

Can't write much tonight as there is nothing worth while to write about. A few more pictures is about the best I can do. These are some more Joe took on his way up here. They were taken from the plane and are some Korean towns as you can see. Namely Taegu and Seoul I imagine.

Today has been a bad one. Has been raining all day and still at it. Guess it is about time for some of the Spring rains though.

Won't write anymore, but will try to send a few more lines tomorrow night along with some more pictures.

Lots of Love,
Bill

Thursday Night

April 30, 1953

9:00 p.m.

Dear Mom & All,

Can check off another day and send a few more pictures. Eventually maybe I will get all of these home and do away with these short notes.

Well, it finally quit raining and today was another beautiful Spring one. Things are really getting green now after all the rain and a little sunshine.

Will try to do better tomorrow night, but this will have to be all for now.

Lots of Love,
Bill

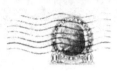

Friday Night

May 1, 1953

9:15 p.m.

Dear Mom & All,

It certainly seems good to be writing May instead of April which means another month has passed. However, the weather is cooler to-night than its been in the last couple of weeks.

Nothing new to write about again tonight as usual. I forgot to men-tion in last night's letter that yesterday was payday. I should have a big increase this month. By the way in case you are wondering what my present salary is now that I'm a Sergeant, $161.24. Maybe I should stay in the Army – Ha!. this will never happen. I would dig ditches first, although I don't think I will have to do that.

Had better pick out a few more pictures and call it quits for tonight.

Lots of Love,
Bill

Saturday Night

May 2, 1953

9:00 p.m.

Dear Mom & All,

Received your nice long letter of the 23rd today. Sure wish I could write a letter to compare with it, but will give out with a few lines tonight and send some more pictures. A couple of more nights and I should get them all home.

You mentioned Joe sending one of the pictures of us. I can't imagine which one it was because I thought I had received them all. Glad he sent it anyway as it beat mine there. The pictures of us together we will both want a print of to keep and remember our wonderful visit in Korea.

I haven't heard from Gene & Marty in sometime, but do hope there is nothing seriously wrong with Gene's back. He has always had trouble with it off and on.

So glad your old friends the Pyles came by to visit with you. Perhaps I have heard you mention them, but can't recall the name. I'm sure you had a lot to talk about after not seeing each other in so many years.

I must say you are doing all right for yourself getting a vacation. Honestly I had forgotten that you had been working there for a year. It hardly seems possible, but then again, if I remember correctly, I was coming home on leave a year ago the 8th of this month.

Yes, the 26th of this month I will have been away for one year, and I imagine Paducah has changed quite a bit. I can hardly wait to see all the latest additions etc. Imagine there will be so many little changes which I will notice. Of course I still picture things as they were when I left.

Joe shouldn't have over a couple of weeks to do over here. I have only had the one letter from him since he returned. Of course he sent the pictures. Maybe he is waiting to give me an estimate on the time he is leaving.

One thing I would like to mention, I am no longer getting the *Sun Democrat*, but there is no need in starting it again. Of course

you did it anyway, but would appreciate clippings of any interest to me.

Had better sign off for this time and sorry I have been so long in writing. Tell all hello and hope all are well.

Lots of Love,
Bill

Monday Night

May 4, 1953

8:45 p.m.

Dear Mom & All,

As you can see, I missed writing last night and sending some more pictures. The reason for this being I had to drive down to Able Battery at 8:30 to take some PX money as the PX Officer was going to Seoul today after rations. It was so late when I returned thought I would wait until tonight to send the remainder of the pictures, this being the last.

Yesterday morning I attended Church Services and enjoyed them as I always do. I like our new Chaplain fine and he is a very good man and worker. The Chaplains over here are doing a good work and help morale 100%.

I think I forgot to mention in my letter the other night about my stopping in Division Headquarters Saturday to see Dewey Ross. He has been down there since December and I pass there every day, but always in too big of a rush to stop. He certainly was glad to see me and I him. We had a nice little talk about old times and where this one and that one was or who we had heard from recently. He also asked about my family.

Guess tomorrow will be another big day and plenty of work as I have to take in the remainder of winter clothing and then take it all down to turn in. Certainly will be glad when all of this is over.

I have been meaning to ask - as you never mention it - have been wondering if Leo is still around. Think you would have told me if anything happened to him, but guess you just don't think about mentioning him. Was just looking at the picture I have of him and wondering if he would remember Joe and me. Had better sign off as I could never fill another page. Want to write Kenneth tonight.

Love to All,

Bill

Saturday Night

May 9, 1953

8:30 p.m.

Dear Mom & All,

After writing so often and sending the pictures, I have really slacked off. I received your letter of the 28th yesterday and as always glad to hear from you. This was the first mail I had received in about a week so it really looked good. Then today I received a nice long letter from Mrs. Potts, plus a picture of herself and Bro. Potts, plus a picture of Clovis' car. She said he wanted a picture of the car, so she sent me one also. I really am proud to have the pictures of them.

Your letter yesterday explained the reason I haven't heard from Joe Ned. I have still only had the one letter since his visit and am a little peeved at him for not writing. I suppose he made R&R as I haven't heard from him. I certainly am glad he got to go as I enjoyed it so much and know he will too. Don't imagine I will make it again before going home.

Well, if I remember correctly one year ago yesterday I came home on leave before coming over. This hardly seems possible, but it makes me feel good anyway and I know my time is getting shorter. Guess these next couple of months will be the longest. I am anxiously awaiting the news of what time Joe is to leave. Shouldn't be too long now.

Tomorrow is Mother's Day and though you may not realize it, I will be thinking of my Mother and how wonderful she has always been. Of course its not only on this day, but every day of the year that we are thankful for having such a sweet Mother and how good she has always been to us. I hope you received the card which I sent.

I don't know what to think about you going to work an hour early one morning. I didn't know you were that much interested in your work! I too laughed when I read it and know how easy it is to do such things. Didn't Dad pull the same trick one time when he was still working for Dudley?

Tell Dad to slow down on those fish! It will be just my luck for him to pull out a bunch when we get to go without me catching a

one. I always said if there were any to be had, he could pull them out when no one else could. Guess Bill Wurtz found this out!

Spring must be officially here! Yesterday I got all the stoves turned in and drew Summer Sleeping Bags. Now have to issue them out to the troops and take in the Mountain Sleeping Bags. This will be the last phase of winter clothing to turn in and will I be glad!

Guess I had better close for now and try to drop Bro. and Mrs. Potts a few lines. They have certainly been good to me and I know they, too, are anxious to hear from Clovis and me. Tell everyone hello for me!

Lots o Love,
Bill

P.S. Incidentally - your letter was the first I have received addressed Sgt. Nace. Thanks for the congratulations.

Wednesday Night

May 13, 1953

9:30 p.m.

Dear Mom & All,

Received your very nice long letter of the 3rd yesterday and as usual enjoyed it very much. Of course I was shocked at the news it bore of Doc's death, but like you said, it is one of those things that happens and none of us have any power over. Yes, I had much rather receive the word of such things while I'm here than to find it out when I get home. I do want you to express my deepest sympathy to Irene and family. I realize it will be very hard for them, but things will work out and go well.

I'm sure you told me about it, but it had slipped my mind that E.B. and Virginia were parents. When was the baby born and what is its name? I can imagine they are happy parents.

I was certainly glad to hear the news about Bubba Lynn. This is something to be proud about. I knew he had thought along this line some time ago. No matter how hard you seem to fight it, or how long it takes you to make up your mind, the Lord will finally overrule you and one realizes, it is this he must do.

Well, today I turned in the last phase of winter clothing which was the arctic sleeping bags. I am glad to get all this over with, but what a day to turn them in, as it is very cool tonight. We all will probably shiver all night due to the sudden change in sleeping gear and then a cool night to top things off.

Day before yesterday I had to go back and pick up a new jeep. It was just like driving a new car back home in comparison with over here. Being supply sergeant I have to see to everything from a 2-1/2, ton truck down to a nail, or at least it has to come through me.

If all goes as planned, Joe will be on his way home in a couple of days. Sure wish I was going with him, but I was still at home when he was in the Army. I didn't have enough time to get a letter back to him after receiving the news of his shipping date, but make him write me after getting home and tell me about the return trip. After all, I let him in on what was in store coming over, and he can do the same for me going back.

It just entered my mind a day or so ago that in a couple of weeks I will be 22 years old. How the time does fly and I can hardly realize that I ought to be this old. I haven't even been home since I have become a man - Ha!

I suppose I had better bring this letter to a close for this time and will try to do a little better on my correspondence. I can truthfully say that you have been grand to write like you have while I have been gone, especially when your time is limited and you have had so many to correspond with. Hoping and trusting all are well.

Lots of Love,
Bill

Sunday Afternoon

May 17, 1953

Dear Mom & All,

Such a beautiful Sunday afternoon, decided to take a few minutes off and answer your letter of the 6th which I received yesterday. Also in yesterday's mail, I had a nice long letter from Earl Nagle. He says his shoulder is coming along fine and he is doing well. Also, said he and Pat Kramer were now engaged, but had not set the wedding date.

As I said at the beginning of the letter, this is really a beautiful day and no one seems to be hurting themselves at working, but then again it is Sunday, though just another day, there is something or some feeling which makes one know it is the Lord's Day, and sets it apart from others. This morning I attended worship services and we even had Layman's Day. One of the fellows in the outfit (a former ministerial student) delivered the message which was very good and everyone enjoyed it so much.

Guess by the time you receive this letter, Joe will be on the high seas headed for home. One of my good buddies also left here on the 15th. I am still keeping my fingers crossed that the points will drop to 38 next month. This will mean the 1st shipment in July for me, other wise it will be the last of July before I leave here. Guess I will do quite a bit more sweating from the Korean heat before I leave.

I wish there was more to write about at this time, while I'm in the mood for writing, but guess this will have to be all for now. Will have to take some more pictures in order to write a little more often. Tell all hello and write when you can.

Lots of Love,
Bill

Thursday Night

May 21, 1953

Dear Mom & All,

A few more days have passed and this finds me trying to think of a few words to write. Everything is going about the same and not much new to write about.

I received your letter of the 11th a couple of days ago and also with it was the box of can goods. I could hardly realize it had time enough to get here since your writing of it being on the way. Thanks so much, but you didn't need to go to the trouble, but then again we are enjoying it. Very much to my surprise I also received a birthday greeting and note from Betty and Ross Morgan.

What can we call the Bloomington Kids now? I certainly was surprised at this news, and hope they are well pleased with the news. At any rate they can get home a little more often. I'm kind of disappointed, because I had planned on seeing their apartment. They were so well pleased with it.

The last couple of days things have been pretty much in a stew with me as we are changing BC's and of course this means a property check, where the new BC sees that all the property we are supposed to have is still on hand and this covers every item.

I would like to write more, but it is pretty late and then again nothing more to write. Thanks again for the nice package and I will write more soon.

Lots of Love,
Bill

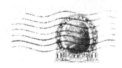

Tuesday Night

8:45 p.m.

Dear Mom & All,

Remember one year ago this morning? I'm sure you too recalled it on this date as I threw a duffel bag on my shoulder and said so long for a while. It makes me feel good to know that one year has now passed since I left home because my time seems much shorter. As I said before, it seems only yesterday so to speak that I said goodbye to you.

Yesterday's mail brought a nice long letter from you plus a birthday cake and card, Mom - you are really wonderful to do such things and never forget. The card was so nice and carried such a sweet message. We are going to try the cake as soon as I finish this letter. There is no doubt in my mind but what it will be good. I would like to save it until the 29th, but had better eat it now, although I believe it would keep as its in perfect condition now.

I also had a short letter from Joe yesterday which was written on the 18th stating he was getting ready to depart Korea once and for all. I hope this true for everyone (excuse this last line as one of the fellows wanted me to try his pen he just received).

I can't recall the Matlocks you spoke of knowing me. Guess it is someone I dealt with while working at the bank. The name sounds familiar. Gee - I'm not going to know the neighborhood around there. New houses, street markers and all. With all of these changes I will probably need the street marker myself to find home - Ha!

Things are as usual with me, and enjoying the pretty weather. Won't be long until I will be saying how hot it is, like I did the cold. Seems we can never be satisfied, but I prefer the warm weather in a place like this.

Nothing more to write about for this time, so will sign off for now.

Lots of Love,
Bill

P.S. Wednesday Morn – 27 May, 8:00 a.m. We finished the cake last night and all really enjoyed it.

Saturday Night

May 30, 1953

8:30 p.m.

Dear Mom & All,

What a nice long letter I received from you today. Really contained the news and just the kind I like to receive. I don't see how you can write such long interesting letters, but they are all just like that,

Well, I am now 22 years old as of yesterday. Really on the upward grade now. I have spent the last couple of birthdays away from home, but hope its the last time I have to do so in the Army. It was just another day of Army life in Korea, but did receive a couple of cards yesterday and one the day before. The two yesterday were from Gene & Marty (with a nice letter on the back) and one from Sue Habacker. The day before brought one from the Potts. I'm surprised so many remembered this date.

It is now 3:00 p.m. Sunday afternoon. Sorry I didn't finish this last night, but some of the boys came in and we got to talking so I had to put off writing until this time.

We are now having one of those good Korean rains. It started sometime in the night and has been at it all day and doesn't show any signs of stopping.

This morning I attended church services, but they were held inside of a tent due to the rain. Also today is the last of the month which means payday in the Army. My pay was boosted quite a bit this month as I pulled $103.00 over the board. One reason for it being so much as I had about ten days of Sergeant pay coming from last month. Ordinarily it will be around $90.00 bucks. This isn't too bad with sending $70.00 a month home which of course is the bond and allotment. If all goes well, I will have only one more payday left in Korea.

What a time I have had finishing this letter. It is now 8:30 and I have just finished my night job of selling. Beings today was payday, I practically sold everything on hand.

One of the Lts who came in the Btry a short while ago asked me the other day if I wasn't from Paducah. He wanted to know if I knew

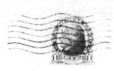

Joe Rogers as he went through OCS with him and they came over together. Said Joe was in the 40th Division.

Incidentally, I had a nice long letter from George Hannin the other day who also landed in the 40th Division. He seems to be doing fine and I was certainly glad to hear from him and receive his address.

Guess I had better bring this letter to an end before something else comes up and I don't get to finish it tonight.

By the way, you run into more people who say they know me and I can't place, of course the latest being Clara Housman McDaniel you spoke of. I can always recognize a face, but hard for me to remember names. Anyway, maybe I'm better known in Paducah than I think - Ha!

Tell everyone hello for me and write when you can.

Lots of Love,
Bill

Friday Night

June 5, 1953

10:15 p.m.

Dear Mom & All,

Guess it is about time I dropped a few lines your way. Just got to thinking, it has been almost a week since I last wrote. Today I received the other nice Birthday Card from you and thought it to be real cute. Also enjoyed all the clippings, but hated to read of Edgar Lovetts death although I had already heard about it. Yesterday I received a very nice B'Day Card from Mrs. Trammel with a short letter enclosed. Really appreciated her thinking of me and wish you would pass on my appreciation to her.

About the only thing that has been any different with me the past week is that day before yesterday I took a trip back to Seoul. A long old rough trip in a 2-1/2 ton truck, but I rather enjoyed it, just getting away from here and seeing a little civilization once more - if that's what you want to call it. My reason for going was that the Battalion PX Officer was going down after rations, so I rode along with him. All the farmers along the way were working in their rice paddies, setting out a new crop. This is really something to see. I remember last fall when I made a trip to Seoul they were all out cutting it.

Today has been a typical summer day and even tonight is rather warm which is very unusual. The days all through the summer are plenty hot, but the nights always cool. Anyway, its pleasant sleeping at the present time after trying to keep warm through the winter.

We have our shower in operation once more, but don't know how long it will last. It really felt good today as the water was warm and I was rather dirty.

By the time you receive this, I hope Joe Ned has made his appearance in Paducah once more. I want you to remind him although I told you before to write and tell me about the homeward voyage. Guess Kenneth will also be home by the time this arrives and Larry keeping busy with work and other activities.

I am enclosing some pictures, which we made around here not too long ago. The ones of me at the typewriter were taken inside the supply

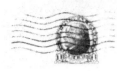

tent. Incidentally, you can tell Joe they were taken with the camera he sold "Smitty."

Guess this will have to be all for now as it is getting rather late and I'm ready to hit the sack. Until next time, hope all is well with everyone at home and write when you can.

Lots of Love,
Bill

Wednesday Night

June 10, 1953

10:00 p.m.

Dear Mom & All,

Seems it is about time I drop a few lines your way once more. I received your letter of the 31st a couple of days ago and should have answered it sooner, but as the time goes by seems that I hate to write letters worse than ever, but then again I still look forward to that wonderful mail, so consequently guess I had better keep up with my correspondence.

Of course the biggest talk around here is the Armistice, and we are all hoping and praying for this to take place. It might mean a little longer stay for me, but this is just a small matter as it would hasten so many more getting home and bring an end to this so called war. Even at that I wouldn't have to stay too much longer as I would come home on ETS. Then again, no one knows what kind of policy will be set up on rotation. All I'm looking for is for it to be over with.

So glad all of you had such a nice trip in Graves County and am sure Aunt Nina and Uncle Ray enjoyed it. Hope there is nothing seriously wrong with Uncle Ray's eyes and he doesn't need an operation.

Sure hope Bro. Turner returns to Ft. Ave. From the last letter I received from the Potts, they talked like they would move. Let me know the outcome on the conference.

Guess Joe is having a wonderful return home about this time. Really looking forward to the day when I can make my appearance. Also suppose Kenneth is out seeking a job.

By the time you receive this it should be around your vacation time, so take it easy and have a good time.

Will write more soon.

Love,
Bill

Dear Mom & All

Tuesday Night

June 17, 1953

11:00 p.m.

Dear Mom & All,

Hope you haven't given me out on letter writing as I know I'm long overdue, but each night have been putting it off until the next and you know how that goes. I will try not to let it happen again.

I received your letter of the 4th a few days ago, telling of your plans to meet Joe Ned. I could hardly believe that he could even be off the water, but getting discharged so rapidly is really going some. I am anxiously awaiting to hear about his trip home etc. I am looking for a letter tomorrow telling of such.

Things are pretty much the same with me and that is one reason I haven't written as there was no news worth telling and I had to write a letter with nothing to say.

Today has been the warmest we have had so far, but I know there are worse coming, as how well I remember the extreme heat of last summer. At any rate, I will say again, I prefer it to the Korean Winters.

We are all still wondering what has become of the Peace Treaty and what the delay seems to be. I am still hoping and praying that it will come soon.

I am enclosing some pictures that were made around the first of the month, which one of the fellows carried on R&R and had developed. These too were made with Joe's old camera and turned out rather well. I am hoping to get a good camera before I get home, while I can get one at a reasonable price. I never did hear whether Joe got another one or not.

I must close for now and will try to write sooner than I did on this one. Tell all hello.

Lots of Love,
Bill

Thursday Night

June 18, 1953

11:00 p.m.

Dear Mom & All,

Received your nice long letter of the 10th today and certainly was glad to hear from you, but I am still missing a letter somewhere as you spoke of Joe writing and telling of his trip home. This letter I have not received and the one I was very anxious to get. This mail situation has been fouled up for sometime so maybe I will get it eventually. I was glad to get the clippings about conference as I wanted to know what changes had been made.

I am glad the Potts received a better position but think maybe they hated to leave Dyersburg. I know everyone there hated to see them go as we did when they left Paducah. I was glad Bro. Turner returned and you can pass on to him how happy I am to have him back. I know everyone was pleased with this.

I can't realize it being so warm at home especially at night. The days are plenty warm here, but the nights and early morning are still very cool.

I certainly hope all your plans work out which you spoke of, meaning all the trips, and that you have a wonderful vacation. You certainly deserve it. Maybe we can make a few more trips when I get home, but I will be satisfied just to stay home for a while.

I have been on the go most of the week running here and there. Always something to take care of, but then again I enjoy just getting out of the area.

This hasn't been much, but thought I had better answer your letter tonight instead of putting it off a night or two like I usually do.

If Larry keeps bringing in all that dough, I may have to hit him up for a loan when I get home. Do you think he would approve of this?

Hope all are well and enjoying the vacations.

Lots of Love,
Bill

Friday Night

June 19, 1953

9:30 p.m.

Dear Mister Nace,

Your letter finally arrived today and I certainly was glad to get the low down on the trip home. I don't know how Mom's letter got here first as it was mailed later. Since I wrote last night stating I hadn't received yours, thought I had better get a few lines off to you tonight and let you know I did receive it.

It must be really great, a civilian once more, boy that sounds good and you can bet I am looking forward to leaving this place. I shouldn't have much over a month now so I can almost count the days.

You might he looking around about the new cars, as I may need your help on what to buy. Of course this is one of the first things I want to do.

I don't know what to think about the Peace Talks and Armistice now. At one time we all thought it was going to be over, but as time goes on the worse things get and the deeper we get involved. I sure wish they would get together on something or the other.

Guess you remember Capek. I had a letter from him yesterday the first since he left and he is now one happy civilian. It took him 33 days to actually reach home. I don't see how you made it so fast. Hope I can be that lucky.

You might be lining up some women for me if they are not all taken or you are too busy with them all - Ha!

Better quit for this time and will write again soon. Tell everyone hello for me.

As Ever,

Bill

Tuesday Night

June 26, 1953

10:15 p.m.

Dear Mom & All,

Guess it is about time I sent a few lines your way. I have been thinking I would receive a letter the last few days and then would write, but suppose I have waited long enough. By my writing tonight I will be sure to get a letter tomorrow.

Also, I slipped up on my dates a little bit. Although I didn't get Birthday Greetings to you in time, nevertheless I thought about it and didn't forget. Please accept a belated greeting and I'm sorry for not getting it there on time. If you remember one year ago yesterday I arrived in Japan, and it also marked the end of three years fighting in Korea. I sure was hoping they wouldn't have to go into four years, but everything seems to be in such a mess now looks as if they are almost back where they started. We are all holding on that maybe something will work out and the end is in store soon.

About the greatest news with me is that I received my first decoration today. Of course it doesn't mean much and don't think I could wear it on a blue suit, but I was rather proud of it anyway. At least it makes me feel that my work was recognized. The Capt. read the Citation this morning at formation and presented me with the medal. I am sending the Citation and Recommendation for Award in a separate envelope which you should receive along with this. Also, I have prepared the medal for mailing which you should receive soon, and are welcomed to open. Just keep them for me as I'm sure you will without doubt.

I am really beginning to look toward the end of my tour over here now. Of course I still have about another month, but as soon as July rolls around, I know it should be sometime in that month. As I said before, if all goes as is, it will be the later part of the month before I leave, so keep writing until you hear my shipping date.

The first part of the week it rained for about three days without stopping. During this time the weather was very cool, but today, has really been one of those Korean Summer days. Guess Summer has officially arrived now.

Looks like this has about covered the latest news with me, so had better be thinking about hitting the old sack. Before too long I can begin thinking about a nice comfortable bed.

Tell all hello and I will try to write again soon.

Lots of Love,
Bill

Monday, June 29, 1953

6:00 p.m.

Dear Mom & All,

As usual not much to write about, but thought I would knock out a few lines just to keep in practice. I received your letter which was written in Gary, and so glad you got to make the trip. I know everyone enjoyed it and only wish that I could have been with you. Like you said, we will try to go again when I return home. I don't know what is wrong with the mail situation around here as it took me eleven days to receive that letter. I was so happy to receive the letter, I didn't even notice the post mark until you mentioned it.

NOW, I do have a bit of news which may be of interest to you. If all goes as planned, I should be in the process of leaving Korea by the time you receive this. However, it doesn't mean that I will get home any sooner than I expected as I have been placed on the East Coast and that is the reason for my leaving so soon. I am supposed to leave the Battery on the 5th. This will be a long old boat ride, but I much prefer it to this place, and the sooner I get out of here the better I will like it. At any rate, I will get to see a lot of places which more than likely I will never have the opportunity to visit again, such as Hawaii, going through the Panama Canal, and I hear maybe Puerto Rica. From what I hear this trip takes about 35 days and we will dock in New York. It really came as a surprise to me when they told me last night, so there isn't any need to write any more after you receive this letter unless something unforeseen comes up and I write you differently. All I'm doing at the present is waiting for that time to come.

I boxed up a few of my belongings which I didn't care to take along with me and mailed them home today. They should arrive shortly before I do, so just hold on to the package and I will open it when I get there. I even mailed it to myself and put Mr. on it. I think I much prefer that to Sgt. Don't you?

Guess this will be about all for now, although it hasn't been much, I think it contains the news you have been waiting for just like me. I will try to write once or twice again before leaving and let you have more details. So much for now.

Lots of Love To All,
Bill

Dear Mom & All

William H. Nace

Going home, the beaches of Honolulu, Hawaii

Printed in the USA
CPSIA information can be obtained
at www.ICGtesting.com
JSHW011417160824
R13664500003B/R136645PG68134JSX00041B/25